Catalysts in Interdisciplinary Education

●   ●   ●   ●   ●   ●

Innovation by Academic Health Centers

This publication was produced with the generous support of the Josiah Macy, Jr. Foundation.

Edited by Denise E. Holmes and Marian Osterweis

Association of Academic Health Centers

The Association of Academic Health Centers (AHC) is a national, non-profit organization comprising more than 100 institutional members in the United States that are the health complexes of major universities. An academic health center consists of an allopathic or osteopathic school of medicine, at least one other health professions school or program, and one or more teaching hospitals. These academic health centers are the nation's primary resources for education in the health professions, biomedical and health services research, and many aspects of patient care.

The AHC seeks to influence public dialogue on significant health and science policy issues, to advance education for health professionals, to promote biomedical and health services research, and to enhance patient care. The AHC is dedicated to improving the health of the people through leadership and cooperative action with others.

The views expressed in this book are those of its authors and do not necessarily represent the views of the board of directors of the Association of Academic Health Centers or the membership at large.

Library of Congress Cataloging-in-Publication-Data
Catalysts in Interdisciplinary Education / Denise E. Holmes and Marian Osterweis, editors
     p.   cm.
     ISBN 1-879694-16-6
        1. Medical education—United States. 2. Academic medical centers—United States. 3. Health care teams—Training of —United States. 4. Interdisciplinary approach in education—United States. I. Holmes, Denise E. II. Osterweis, Marian.

     R745.C33 1999   99-046248
     610' 71'173—dc21   CIP

Copies of this book are available from:
Association of Academic Health Centers
1400 Sixteenth Street, N.W., Suite 720
Washington, D.C. 20036
Telephone: 202/265-9600
Fax 202/265-7514
www.ahcnet.org
Price: US$25.00 (plus US$5.00 shipping/handling)

Design and production by Fletcher Design
Copy editor, SSR, Incorporated

Contents

Contributing Authors

Bruce A. Behringer, MPH, is assistant vice president and executive director, Office of Rural and Community Health, East Tennessee State University.

Janis P. Bellack, PhD, RN, FAAN, is associate provost for education and professor of nursing, Medical University of South Carolina.

Wilsie S. Bishop, DPA, is dean, College of Public and Allied Health, East Tennessee State University.

Judith Booker, MEd, is assistant vice president for planning, The University of Texas—Houston Health Science Center.

Linda Brannon, MEd, is assistant vice president for academic affairs, The University of Texas-Houston Health Science Center.

Maria C. Clay, PhD, is codirector, Office of Interdisciplinary Health Sciences Education, associate professor of family medicine and director, Office of Clinical Assessment and Education, East Carolina University.

Charles O. Cranford, DDS, is vice chancellor, University of Arkansas for Medical Sciences.

Doyle M. Cummings, PharmD, FCP, FCCP, is codirector, Office of Interdisciplinary Health Sciences Education; professor of family medicine and director, Research Division, East Carolina University; and clinical professor of pharmacy, University of North Carolina.

Norman H. Edelman, MD, is vice president, Health Sciences Center, and dean, School of Medicine, State University of New York at Stony Brook.

Joellen B. Edwards, PhD, is dean, College of Nursing, East Tennessee State University.

Adolfo Firpo, MD, is former chancellor, University of Puerto Rico Medical Sciences Campus.

Ronald D. Franks, MD, is vice president for health affairs and dean, James H. Quillen College of Medicine, East Tennessee State University.

Vincent A. Fulginiti, MD, is former chancellor, University of Colorado Health Science Center.

Raymond S. Greenberg, MD, PhD, is vice president, academic affairs, and provost, Medical University of South Carolina.

James A. Hallock, MD, is vice chancellor for health sciences and dean, School of Medicine, East Carolina University.

Denise E. Holmes, JD, MPH, is director, Center for Interdisciplinary, Community-Based Learning, and liaison to the American International Health Alliance, Association of Academic Health Centers.

Yvonne L. Lewis, EdD, is associate director of education for the Arkansas Area Health Education Centers (AHEC) Program.

M. David Low, MD, PhD, is president, The University of Texas—Houston Health Science Center.

Chris Mansfield, PhD, is associate professor of family medicine and director, Center for Health Sciences Research and Development, East Carolina University.

Marian Osterweis, PhD, is executive vice president and director, Division of Global Health, Association of Academic Health Centers.

Ann W. Richmond, PhD, is vice dean for academic affairs and faculty development, School of Medicine, State University of New York at Stony Brook.

Harry P. Ward, MD, is chancellor, University of Arkansas for Medical Sciences.

Peter C. Williams, JD, PhD, is professor of preventive medicine and head, Division of Medicine in Society, School of Medicine, State University of New York at Stony Brook.

James C. Wohlleb is assistant director of the Arkansas Area Health Education Centers (AHEC) Program.

What is Past is Prologue: Interdisciplinarity at the Turn of the Century

Denise E. Holmes, JD, MPH, and
Marian Osterweis, PhD

Can it be that in his words from *The Tempest*, William Shakespeare was prophetically describing interdisciplinary health professions education in the United States? Here, at the conclusion of the twentieth century, past may well be prologue, for we are today experiencing a flourishing of interdisciplinarity in health professions education that builds upon and expands past history. This phenomenon begs for closer examination and careful evaluation. Hence, we offer this book so we can delve more deeply into the surrounding circumstances and experiences from across the nation and, ultimately, the lessons that can be derived from success stories.

Catalysts in Interdisciplinary Education: Innovation by Academic Health Centers is a set of case studies on interdisciplinary health professions education at seven member institutions of the Association of Academic Health Centers (AHC) toward the end of the twentieth century. Together, they comprise that snapshot in time when many of our nation's health science centers are seeking new opportunities and strengthening the foundation for collaborative educational efforts.

AHC is producing this publication because we want to explore the burgeoning *institutional* focus on interdisciplinarity, in contrast to many prior works with a *programmatic* emphasis. By doing so, we share instances of academic health centers whose leaders have thought through genuine culture change and are making interdisciplinary experiences a valued, sometimes even a required, part of their students' education.

For several decades, the trend in health professions education was largely toward further subspecialization, which merely engendered further fragmentation, not simply between the individual health professions schools but down to the departmental level. Accordingly, there is a need for institutional leadership from the top that, to effect change, champions opportunities for interdisciplinary activity. The stories in this book illustrate this institutional force at work.

Why is there such broad interest in interdisciplinary health professions education today? Both internal and external influences and pressures drive this trend. As several of the case studies exemplify, many of the conditions that bolstered an escalation of interdisciplinary health professions education in the 1960s and 1970s have reappeared two decades later. For example, the Federal government and philanthropic organizations are again devoting financial resources to efforts that will enhance the quality of care and shore up the health infrastructure in underserved urban and rural areas throughout the nation. Among the steps being taken are providing expanded training opportunities and practice opportunities for local nurses and other health professionals who then must work together in new ways to care for patients.

Health care has a powerful history of team practice with roots in efforts to deliver quality patient services.

Because managed care has radically altered the delivery of health care services, including often dramatic alterations in the roles and practice patterns of health care providers, the education of future health professionals must take the new marketplace realities into account. Reports and recommendations of the Pew Commission, which highlight the need for teamwork and interdisciplinarity among the required competencies for health professionals, have been received and acted upon by many institutions; they are discussed in a number of the papers. Finally, many health science centers face economic pressures that have encouraged them to seek to streamline efforts where possible; combining students from different health professions schools may maximize faculty capacity.

However, this activity in interdisciplinary education is hardly just a retro trend. Health care has a powerful history of team practice with roots in efforts to deliver quality patient services. In hospitals and later in ambulatory clinical settings, health professionals have needed to rely upon people with different training and different skill sets, yet the collaborative blend of skills and qualities among the various providers produced the best care for their patients.

As biomedical science advances and clinicians' foci become even more subspecialized, the lone practitioner has been increasingly less able to handle all of the patient's complex needs. Rather, it is the clear understanding of the contribution of other types of practitioners, together with the ability to combine forces, that can

2

best ensure the desired outcome: a patient's optimal health. This is particularly true for patients with complex conditions, such as those with chronic disease, geriatric patients, or those requiring rehabilitative services. Only a set of practitioners can adequately meet their needs. Where better to learn about and begin to appreciate the contribution of other members of the health care team than during one's professional education?

The history of interdisciplinarity is particularly rich in community-based programs in rural areas. Several institutions profiled here have long striven to combine students from different health professions schools, particularly during their clinical training. Often in large part, this interdisciplinary approach was decided on because no other strategy seemed logical or practical given the community to be served. The University of Arkansas for Medical Sciences (UAMS) and East Carolina University (ECU) are two such institutions. The reader should note that Area Health Education Centers (AHECs) have played an important, integral role in the work of each of these institutions—as they have among others.

In any field, profession, or culture, language is crucial to successful communication and to ensure that all involved are working toward a common goal rather than at cross-purposes. Yet seeking, agreeing upon, and sharing a common language for collaboration among the health professions remains a major challenge. Among the most frequently utilized words used to describe didactic and clinical education involving students from more than one health professions school or program, or to describe initiatives spearheaded by faculty or practitioners from more than one health profession, are *interdisciplinary, interprofessional, multidisciplinary,* and *multiprofessional.* These words are often used interchangeably. People also refer to *cross-professional* and *transdisciplinary* ventures. Vincent Fulginiti, MD, bemoans the sloppiness inherent in lumping these terms together because it thereby gives short shrift to their individual richness. And, indeed, the authors of several papers in this book carefully explicate how they use these terms, offering instruction as to how the reader might choose to distinguish among them. The title of this book uses the word *interdisciplinary,* which is also the word selected for the name of the center under whose auspices this volume was written.*

Notwithstanding the language difficulties, a wide array of other barriers continues to hinder interdisciplinary education and interprofessional collaboration. As Fulginiti declares in his essay, structural and attitudinal hurdles remain. Fortuitously, Fulginiti also offers several suggestions for surmounting these barri-

---

*The Center for Interdisciplinary, Community-Based Learning is a joint project of the Association of Academic Health Centers and the Health Resources and Services Administration of the U.S. Department of Health and Human Services.

ers, such as building on existing institutional and community resources where possible or starting from scratch when necessary. A Web-based course at UAMS is an excellent model for erasing an oft-encountered major obstacle: scheduling. In the same way, each of the other case studies offers examples of homegrown, successful solutions to barriers, together with lessons for others seeking to initiate or facilitate interdisciplinary programs.

The flourishing of such efforts on any given campus requires not only leadership at the top of the academic health center, but also a commitment from all other levels as well. Adolfo Firpo, MD, the former chancellor of the University of Puerto Rico Medical Sciences Campus (MSC-UPR), sets forth principles of visionary leadership. Synthesizing two earlier approaches, he also offers a new definition of the type of leadership that health sciences centers need in the current environment. In addition, Firpo shares several vignettes that illustrate the successful ways in which the previously fragmented faculty, administrators, and staff have contributed to institutional cohesiveness at MSC-UPR. In contrast to this institution, which developed an atmosphere of unity following the arrival of a catalyst in the person of a dynamic leader, the health sciences center at the State University of New York (SUNY) at Stony Brook originally possessed leadership with a collaborative vision, then saw such collaboration become fragmented along the way; it is now striving to return to its collaborative roots.

One way in which leadership can be expressed is with the establishment of a high-profile interdisciplinary office or center within the office of, or reporting to, the vice president for health affairs, chancellor, or vice chancellor. Such a step signifies to all, whether on campus or in the surrounding community, that collaboration across the professions is important to the institutional leadership. East Tennessee State University (ETSU) created an Office of Rural and Community Health, governed by a seven-member board that included the three health science deans and four community representatives. Also in this regard is the work of the Office of Professional Education at the University of Colorado Health Sciences Center, which Fulginiti cites.

As this book was going to press, James A. Hallock, MD, vice chancellor for health sciences and dean of the School of Medicine at ECU, announced the establishment of a new ECU Office of Interdisciplinary Health Sciences Education. Situated at the level of the entire Division of Health Sciences (School of Medicine, School of Nursing, School of Allied Health Sciences), this office will facilitate cross-professional interaction. Its visibility is an important illustration of the underlying message of this book—namely, we appear to be, at the very least, on the brink of a national shift to institutional endorsement of interdisciplinarity in health professions education.

Clearly any such effort at the individual institutional level must receive the endorsement of the deans and faculty throughout the institution, and the reader will glimpse successful approaches throughout this book. Firpo sets out strategies for ensuring the active participation and commitment of these key stakeholders. At the Medical University of South Carolina (MUSC), a deans' council has crafted a list of assumptions and recommendations designed to support the interdisciplinary underpinnings of the institution's strategic plan. Several other authors comment on the need for further faculty training in order to maximize the value of interdisciplinary experiences.

In the chapters that follow, several institutions discuss having been engaged in or now participating in a process of strategic planning that incorporates issues of interdisciplinary education. MUSC presents its forward-looking, university-wide process begun in 1997; its self-examination resulted in an institutional adoption of core competencies across the health professions and incorporation of the AHC Health Professions Covenant into its orientation program for new students. Based on the work of its Inter-Professional Education Development Task Force, established in 1998, UAMS is now considering the value of a department of inter-professional studies. The University of Texas (UT)-Houston shares with our readers the careful deliberation it has just completed and the fruit it expects the work of its task force on core curriculum to bear.

Yet another thread running throughout many of the stories in this volume is the reaching out to other academic institutions to establish partnerships that build on each other's strengths. UT-Houston, which lacked programs in social work, education, and chaplaincy, successfully approached the University of Houston, which boasted such programs, ultimately enhancing the educational experience for all students from both sides of this collaboration. MUSC relied upon its long-standing relationship with the University of South Carolina in Columbia. Perhaps most dramatically—at least in terms of geographical scope— UAMS in 1994 launched an affiliation with the Tulane University School of Public Health and Tropical Medicine that could develop joint institutional endeavors and offer students in Arkansas an opportunity to obtain the master of public health degree.

Is there such an entity as a core curriculum? Different institutions have different takes on this query. Various approaches described here run the gamut yet offer abundant wisdom. ETSU developed a core curriculum for its three health professions schools, including interdisciplinary teaching teams. SUNY Stony Brook developed an elective interdisciplinary course that it envisions as the precursor to a new core curriculum. At MUSC, students from each of three colleges take required courses (interdisciplinary in nature) that are part of their respective college's core curriculum. UAMS's task force preferred instead to consider opportunities for students and faculty without creating an explicit set of core courses. These examples suggest that homegrown solutions are often best, since they incorporate local history, culture, and realities.

In some instances, the number of students or faculty involved in an institution's interdisciplinary efforts remains relatively small and might be prematurely dismissed as less than an institutional commitment to interdisciplinarity. A devil's advocate might point out, for example, that while SUNY Stony Brook offers a detailed description of its expanding commitment to shared competencies across the health professions, its story, in essence, is of a lone course taught in the spring of 1999. Nonetheless, the SUNY Stony Brook account is replete with lessons, given the large number of faculty involved, the novel approach for determining the mix of students from the various schools (each of the five schools selected ten students), and the level of planning needed to counter common objections (e.g., the question of negligible faculty rewards).

Looking ahead, what do these stories collectively portend for the future of interdisciplinarity in health professions education? Together, they may well represent the emergence of a trend in which numerous forces have conspired to produce a rare yet pronounced shift in the way that future health professionals are educated. We may be at the dawn of an era of a national pledge to institutional interdisciplinarity. It is noteworthy to mention that several European nations and Japan have progressed more rapidly than has the United States with regard to interprofessional collaboration. Although these other national experiences are beyond the scope of this volume, our increasingly interconnected, globalized health care community suggests that we will continue to learn from our neighbors in other lands. Perhaps as the world proceeds to shrink, U.S. institutions will catch up with their more progressive counterparts elsewhere.

It remains to be seen whether an interdisciplinary approach will ultimately be deemed the appropriate way to educate future health professionals. In the long term, we will need evaluative research to demonstrate whether interdisciplinary education enriches the educational experience, produces better health professionals, and enhances patient care. However, the anecdotal evidence presented in this volume points in that direction. What is past is prologue, and the future's prologue is here today.

The Right Issue at the Right Time

Vincent A. Fulginiti, MD

The art of medicine in Egypt is thus exercised: one physician is confined to the study and management of one disease; there are of course a great number who practice this art; some attend to the disorders of the eyes, others to those of the head, some take care of the teeth, others are conversant with all diseases of the bowels; whilst many attend to the care of maladies which are less conspicuous.

—Herodotus (484–424 B.C.)

ANYWHERE, 1999–2000 AND BEYOND

Bobby Smith, a two-month-old child, is brought to his pediatrician because of persistent vomiting. Bobby and his parents are seen by the receptionist, Ms. Price, who logs them in, prepares the chart, and introduces them to Ms. Walters, Dr. Briggs's child health associate/physician assistant. She takes Bobby's history, weighs and measures him, records his vital signs, and conducts a preliminary examination during which she notes a mild upper respiratory infection with cloudy nasal discharge. After the examination, Ms. Walters consults with Dr. Briggs and his nurse, who then attend the child. Dr. Briggs, using Ms. Walters's trusted data, examines Bobby. He becomes concerned that, although the child may have an initial episode of food intolerance or allergy, he also could have a more serious condition. Dr. Briggs counsels Mrs. Smith about dietary restrictions and says he wants to see Bobby in two days if the child's condition does not improve.

Two days later Bobby's runny nose has cleared, but he is now experiencing projectile vomiting. His mother brings him back to Dr. Briggs, who repeats the procedures he performed on the previous visit. This time, both Ms. Walters and Dr. Briggs suspect pyloric stenosis, an obstruction of the exiting area of the stomach that prevents food from entering the small bowel.

Dr. Briggs refers the Smiths to Dr. Walsh, an expert pediatric surgeon, to whom Dr. Briggs outlines his findings and suspicion of pyloric stenosis. At Dr. Walsh's office, the nurse, Mrs. Kline, takes the referral history, performs a preliminary evaluation and vital sign examination, and introduces the Smiths to Dr. Walsh. Dr. Walsh examines Bobby, and she confirms the probable presence of pyloric stenosis although Bobby's case lacks the classical findings. Dr. Walsh asks Mrs. Kline and the receptionist, Mr. Jameson, to arrange for a hospital admission for evaluation and possible surgical correction of the lesion.

After preliminary registration at the hospital, the Smiths are escorted to the pediatric ward where a nurse, Ms. Flores, and a nursing assistant greet them and settle Bobby in his room. They discuss Bobby with his parents to ensure that any special needs and concerns are noted, and then prepare Bobby for radiological confirmation of the suspected diagnosis. Ms. Flores inserts an intravenous line according to the orders received, and administers appropriate fluids. Prior to establishing the fluid flow, a specimen of blood is obtained and urine collected and sent to the hospital laboratory, where Mr. Spence performs the required tests. He reports the results back to the ward.

In the meantime, Bobby is sent to radiology, where Ms. Anglethorpe prepares him for an upper GI study. Dr. Chang reads the completed radiographs as consistent with pyloric stenosis, and communicates his findings to Doctors Walsh and Briggs. Dr. Walsh confirms with Dr. Briggs that surgery is indicated and arranges for the procedure.

After fluid correction, Bobby is taken to the operating room and the pyloric stenosis is identified and corrected. Bobby has an uneventful recovery.

WHAT IS INTERPROFESSIONAL EDUCATION?

The clinical situation described above occurs reasonably frequently in pediatrics. The scenario illustrates the number of health professionals and other persons involved in caring for a "simple" pyloric stenosis. Perhaps Dr. Briggs and Dr. Walsh attended to the problem without overtly recognizing the host of others who participated in Bobby Smith's care. This example is but one of thousands that occur every day involving routine to exceptional health care. But the scenario demonstrates that health professionals who enter the workplace after completing their education often learn quickly that they must team with other health professionals.

In Bobby Smith's case, many highly trained people were involved in his care. Yet the education of many of these professionals often takes place in monolithic, isolated institutions whose disciplinary approaches do not require knowledge of or work with other health professionals. This discrepancy between isolated academic preparation and the realities of the professional world has led many health professions educators to re-examine their curricular approach, bringing about a new emphasis on interdisciplinary education.

Some consider the term "interdisciplinary" less than satisfactory to describe their efforts. As a result, a plethora of terms has evolved, including multidisciplinary, interdepartmental, cross-disciplinary, interprofessional, and multiprofessional. Research tools such as Internet search engines show the range of other terms used in the literature. DeWitt Baldwin (1996) has suggested the term "interdisciplinary" to designate undergraduate education, and "interprofessional" to indicate education that involves only health professionals. In this paper, I will use interprofessional throughout (in Baldwin's sense) to signify a focus on health professional education.

BARRIERS TO INTERPROFESSIONAL EDUCATION

One might think that the reality of the workplace would determine the reality of the curriculum. Sadly, health professions educators, because they focus on communicating information about a specific discipline and not on practicing that discipline, have not necessarily paid attention to the skills needed in team care. Viewing health care educators, whether in academic institutions or other teaching venues, as if they are "monks" or "nuns" provides a useful metaphor for this phenomenon. In the cloistered atmosphere in which they teach, their focus tends to be narrow, limited to their profession's concerns. They do not consider the community's needs; some feel doing so would contaminate the academic environment in which they wish students to learn. It is as if they were doing God's work and therefore need not be concerned with what is happening in the real world outside the academic institution. Intrusion of community concerns or the real workplace that their students will enter might be too practical and not sufficiently theoretical. In many instances, this results in a separation between the teaching center and the community, one aspect of the so-called town-gown problem. Others have described and analyzed this situation (Baldwin 1998; Gordon and Kipnis 1999; Hensel et al. 1996; Mennin and Kalishman 1998; Sataloff 1998).

Consequently, and despite the obvious need for health professionals to work together and understand something about each other's fields, curricular content and structure follow strict disciplinary lines. The products of such monolithic education are often ill-prepared for the reality of professional teamwork unless they instinctively sense the value of cooperation and collegiality (COGME 1997; Simon et al. 1999).

Monolithic education often presents examples and principles of an isolated professional role, rather than cooperative ones. Many managed care organizations have recently discovered this fact, and some claim that it takes months to a year or more to integrate an individual health professional into the true team relationships that health care requires (COGME 1997). One aspect of this lack of preparation is an attitudinal problem that makes it difficult for the sole-provider mindset to adapt to care by a host of health professionals, each with a vital role in truly caring for the patient.

There is great reluctance to examine current curricular efforts with an eye to eliminating some content to make room for desirable insertions, such as interprofessional courses.

Apart from the narrow disciplinary perspective, other influences encourage monolithic instruction (Bulger and Bulger 1990). Some are structural, intrinsic to the organization of academic health centers or other teaching institutions; some are attitudinal (Commission on Medical Education 1992; Shuster and Reynolds 1998). One example of a structural influence is the very organization of teaching institutions. These institutions, most often academic health centers, are monolithic; their professional schools are separately housed, with duplicate educational space, duplicate faculty in various subdisciplines, and disparate clinical arenas in which students gain direct patient experience. For example, a school of medicine might have its students located in a university hospital and affiliated clinics, whereas students at the schools of nursing, dentistry, and pharmacy learn at separate clinical sites.

Professional schools other than medicine often enter into the community to find faculty and patient contact, but university sites bar them because of limited patient contact time, real or imagined. In some instances, the clinical site functions as if it were affiliated solely with the school of medicine, thereby automatically giving medical students primacy. Whatever the reason, these disparities lead to isolated student learning without the presence of students from other disciplines.

Another set of structural problems encourages isolation: Schools have different time periods of instruction (semesters, trimesters, quarters, etc.), class length, and class size. This leads to the inability to schedule students simultaneously. Not surprisingly, faculty who adhere to the monolithic model seize upon these differences in schedules to discourage interprofessional courses instead of seeking solutions that enable interprofessional contact and education.

Finally, the physical structure of many of our professional schools lacks both lecture halls for large classes and small-group rooms for problem-based or other instruction for small groups. All of these physical constraints can be overcome by a diligent faculty and administration set on modifying the learning experience appropriately.

One serious attitudinal barrier has become embedded in the professional reward system in most of our academic health centers. Promotion and tenure decisions are largely based on rewarding faculty for their research productivity, despite claims to the contrary. Teaching is considered by most institutions as necessary but not sufficient for such decisions. Clinical productivity has its own reward system of higher income and incentives. But innovation in teaching and the scholarly effort required to undertake such activities as designing and implementing an interprofessional course most often go unrewarded. In fact, these efforts may work against career enhancement. By focusing intense intellectual effort on such worthy activities, a faculty member may find that he or she is rated poorly in other areas, despite spectacular achievement in this one.

In addition, and sadly, many professions are disdainful or envious of others; this disdain often leads to an isolationist policy based on political or turf considerations and not on sound educational principles. Other attitudinal influences include disparity in student age, prior experience or education, and levels of maturity in science that limit the ability to bring students from different disciplines together in a single classroom or clinical encounter; often, a strong belief exists among some educators that interprofessional offerings are soft sciences that distract from important content and dilute time in their own disciplinary curriculum. There is great reluctance to examine current curricular efforts with an eye to eliminating some content to make room for desirable insertions, such as interprofessional courses.

Finally, many believe that interprofessional education—and other educational changes—are fads and that fads come and go; traditional curricula survive the test of time.

Up to this point, I have generalized about dominant themes in many of our institutions of professional education. Of course, isolation does not occur in every institution, nor in every part of an institution. Many programs do bring together students from diverse disciplines. One obvious instance is the Area Health Education Center (AHEC) concept. One of its intrinsic principles is to bring together students from multiple disciplines at clinical sites to work with various kinds of community practitioners. In many instances, it works extremely well; in others, structural and attitudinal hurdles prevent full realization of the concept. In some academic health centers, interprofessional doctoral programs begin with such courses as "Introduction to Health Care" or "Preparation for Clinical Medicine."

Despite all the negative influences, however, modern educators have felt the need to pursue interprofessional efforts and, in some measure, they have succeeded (Baldwin 1998; Fagin 1992; Goldberg 1995; Sataloff 1998; Singleton and Green-Hernandez 1998). (The case studies in this book describe a number of these efforts.)

WHY INTERPROFESSIONAL EDUCATION

Just as interprofessional care is not new, so interprofessional education has a long history. Baldwin (1996, 1998) has covered this area exhaustively, but for our purposes, a brief summary will suffice.

Educators in the United States and abroad have made many attempts to institute this logical method of educating health professionals. Some techniques are no longer viable while some have survived, modified to accommodate faculty perceptions and schedules. Others have thrived and continue to expand in innovative ways. Many have been initiated, stimulated, and funded by such organizations as the Health Resources and Services Administration (HRSA) within the U.S. Department of Health and Human Services (in 1988), the W.K. Kellogg Foundation (in 1991), the Robert Wood Johnson Foundation (in 1992), and the Pew Commission (in 1995), all with strong emphasis on interprofessional education and practice.

Original programs began early in this century and experienced a revival in the 40s and 50s with a focus on primary family care and preventive medicine. Many disappeared as the era of the specialist appeared, which tended to downplay integration and emphasize isolated care. In the 60s, as the neighborhood health center concept took hold, multiprofessional teams were assembled in these units to deliver care, largely to the indigent population. Private care continued to follow the more traditional mode of isolated care. Often with Federal support, some programs have evolved into community health centers with considerable local citizen impact.

Another resurgence occurred in the 80s under the aegis of the then-U.S. Veterans Administration, when interprofessional teams were instituted to care for the aging veteran population. Remnants of this effort persist and have expanded to include interdisciplinary teams in geriatrics. Today, many academic health centers are again considering interprofessional education in response to both the external environment and internal education innovation.

For many reasons, a portion of all health professions education must today address interprofessional issues. These include the following:

1. Understanding and appreciating the roles of health professionals— Patient care, for the most part, is delivered by teams, not by individuals. In contrast to the monolithic, ancient Egyptian method, the care of Bobby Smith illustrates that care for a "simple" condition included the skills of a pediatric child health associate, a pediatrician, a surgical office nurse, a pediatric surgeon, an in-patient surgical nurse and her assistant, a laboratory technician, a radiology technician, and a radiologist. The team members, to practice evidence-based medicine effectively, must work together with full knowledge of each other's appropriate roles and priorities and of the nature and timing of each intervention. True teamwork cannot occur in the absence of such knowledge, except by happenstance. Lack of intersection can, and too often does, result in inconvenient, costly, inappropriate, or even dangerous care.

2. Achieving maximum efficiency of patient contact and delivering the maximum quantity of health care cost-effectively—Patients, the marketplace, and academe all now focus on quality care delivered in a cost-conscious environment; teamwork offers such attributes (Buckle et al. 1999; Caplan et al. 1992; Egan and Jewler 1997; Lavoie and Kaplowitz 1996; Reitan 1996; Sataloff 1997; Stair 1998). Consider what might have happened if Bobby's caretakers had applied the wrong techniques to diagnose and treat him. Surgery might have been delayed, his fluid and electrolyte balance might have become dangerously deranged, and his life could have been jeopardized.

3. Keeping faculty time and teaching space within health educational institutions productive while using both efficiently—Never before in the history of health care have faculty experienced such claims on their time and productivity. Changes in the health care system demand that patient care be patient centered, of high quality, and efficiently delivered without excessive use of laboratory, hospital, or consultant resources (Gordon and Kipnis 1999). Use of teamwork in health professional institutions helps ensure such successful health care in today's environment. The days of the solo practitioner are gone, if they ever truly existed.

4. Making those academic subjects that are common to all health professionals available to all students—All health professions students need a basic understanding of anatomy, physiology, biochemistry, pathology, pharmacology, and the other basic sciences. Why teach them separately in each professional school on the same campus? Such inefficient use of faculty time and effort detracts from other productive faculty activity. Why not try to find ways to economize and teach all of the information to all students at a given level, irrespective of their health professions school?

5. Encouraging contributions from a variety of disciplines in order to understand complex issues in patient care—The clinical scenario that I offered at the beginning of this essay is relatively straightforward. I might have illustrated the point with a complicated genetic disease requiring the joint care of practitioners in multiple disciplines and subdisciplines. Complex diseases or conditions cry out for integrated care by the various health providers, with full use of teamwork. The nurse, primary physician, geneticist, genetic counselor, technician, social worker, physical therapist, and other specialists may be required to develop and implement a comprehensive plan for the best outcome. Teamwork is not only desirable; it is mandatory. Where better to start than in the health professional's early education?

6. Delivering all of the needed aspects of other health care that a single health care provider cannot offer in isolation—Although this concept should be obvious, it is often overlooked in the education of health care providers. Shouldn't a neurologist have extensive knowledge and understanding of what a physical therapist can do for patients? Shouldn't a family medicine physician know what a social worker is capable of providing for patients? Shouldn't a nurse practitioner know what a laboratory technician is able to do for patients? More important, shouldn't all of these health care providers know that they cannot deliver care alone? That knowledge should be one solid objective of interprofessional education.

7. Stimulating interaction between health professions students, which can lead to greater trust and healthier interactions in the clinical arena—This is one way to overcome the barrier of disdain for or envy of other health care professionals. Students working together in the classroom or clinical setting will have greater respect for each other because they will react to individuals rather than to labels. The latter often occurs in the monolithic educational mode where interaction is limited to a few clinical areas. And some interaction is more apparent than real; does a medical student really know what a pharmacist does, even if the resident or attending physician asks him or her to write a prescription?

8. Sharing the standards of care that are becoming the rationale for effective delivery among all health professionals caring for the patient—There is no separate provider-patient relationship for each profession. We all share the same ethical, humanistic, and legal duties to our patients. Why, then, do we task students to learn these elements in isolation? Why not have them learn together so that the bond between the team of health care providers and the patient is woven from a single strand, not a patchwork of different professional standards?

9. Aiding education in practice for health professions students and providing continuing education for the health professions preceptor by teamwork in action—There is no better way to overcome the barriers than with elbow-to-

elbow educational contact. One learns as one perceives; if the team is the teacher, the concept is validated.

Some critics may cite the lack of proof that interprofessional education is necessary or results in better care. It is true that at present we can only cite the multiple rationales that suggest such education is beneficial and needed. We may not have all of the necessary rigorous clinical and educational proof that the outcome improves patient care, but some evidence does exist. Improved educational performance, quality of care, and attitudinal change have all been documented (Baldwin 1994; Blue et al. 1998; Curley et al. 1998; DePoy et al. 1997; Gordon et al. 1996; Hayward et al. 1996; O'Neil 1993; Ray 1998; Wartmann et al. 1998).

Nevertheless, there should be increased effort to document the outcome of these interprofessional educational enterprises and to evaluate their effectiveness. At present, we operate on the premise that teamwork in managed care and other settings appears to demand a different mindset and different set of skills than our current graduates demonstrate when they enter the clinical arena. The fact that re-education appears to be necessary implies that the monolithic mode of health professional education does not serve the real world of health care.

STRATEGIES FOR INTERPROFESSIONAL EDUCATION

If interprofessional education is to succeed in an academic health center environment traditionally committed to monolithic education, educators must seek a satisfactory venue in which to initiate and perpetuate interprofessional learning. There are a variety of methods that may be used in such settings. Some examples appear below.

Utilizing Existing AHECs

AHECs, which provide clinical arenas for education at multiple sites distant from the home institution offer an almost ideal environment for the clinical components of an interprofessional experience. Multiple health professionals can be recruited from local providers and, if combined with visiting faculty from the main campus, can provide a rich interprofessional environment. Team care—and education for such care—is facilitated in an arena in which health professionals perform their functions as part of an integrated team, not as isolated providers.

Baldwin (1998) has stressed that teamwork is the best model for learning, since it immediately and intrinsically demonstrates the value of each professional's skills; patients benefit from an integrated, rather than fragmented, approach.

Locating all the health professionals at the site ensures multiple, ongoing channels of communication and constant emphasis on each provider's role in the care of a specific patient.

Another advantage for planners is the potential to adapt the interprofessional model to an existing environment, in contrast to having to establish a new set of interprofessional arrangements.

Utilizing an Existing Interdisciplinary or Interprofessional Course

In some academic health centers, an established course can provide the framework for expansion into a true interprofessional curriculum. That is the model I advocated for the University of Colorado Health Sciences Center when I served as chancellor. We established three separate interprofessional courses: programs in "Genetics," "Geriatrics," and "Health Care Ethics, Law, and Humanities," all instituted since 1993. They are managed by the Deans' Council, with a lead dean for each program dealing with day-to-day matters. Although I believed that the "Geriatrics" program lent itself most readily to interprofessional education, our Deans' Council initiated the course work with the program in "Health Care Ethics, Law, and Humanities." This choice has precedents, and also has been successful since its initiation in 1995 (Browne et al. 1995; Kent 1997).

The first course, which starts the academic year, consists of an orientation for all doctoral students in each of our five professional schools. The program subsequently introduced a course in biomedical ethics, initially for medical students but now including students from nursing, medicine, physical therapy, and the child health associate/physician's assistant programs. This ten-week course encompasses small, didactic, once-weekly sessions, and involves both the full-time ethics faculty and more than fifty of the interprofessional faculty. It will be expanded to include dental and pharmacy students next year.

Geriatrics appears to be a logical rubric for interprofessional education. All health professionals must cooperate in the care of the elderly, who make up a large part of the health care burden, especially for chronic disease and especially requiring the services of multiple health professionals. All students should learn such topics as the aging process, the immunology of aging, the common disease processes that afflict the elderly, the social factors in elder care, the financial challenges, the physical attributes of aging, and health care at the end of life. All of these issues cross disciplines. Whatever the course chosen, an institution can build up to a greater interprofessional presence in the curriculum by incrementally adding small didactic, interactive group discussions and clinical encounters.

One advantage of this method is the existing cadre of faculty and students familiar with the mingling of professional students. They can act as catalysts for continuing development and as advocates for the concept. The role that early adapters can play in advocacy for interprofessional education cannot be emphasized adequately.

Utilizing a Community Resource

It may be possible for some educational institutions to elicit the help and cooperation of local facilities that practice interprofessionally. For example, in many communities, Federally accredited community health centers follow the interprofessional mode. With cooperative planning, and with the academic health center supplying additional resources in the form of financial support and faculty effort, it may be possible to layer an interprofessional educational opportunity onto the already extant clinical activity. The advantages to both entities may be found in better continuing education by the admixture of academic and community personnel, stronger ties and understanding between town and gown, opportunities for clinical partnering in a highly competitive external environment, and stronger community support for both entities. Many rural sites are adaptable for such interprofessional education. These might be part of an Area Health Education Center or an academic health center, or they can be developed selectively and separate from any other organizational structure, depending on local circumstances.

Starting From Scratch

Many academic health centers simply do not have the history or tradition of even rudimentary interprofessional education. For these institutions, it is necessary to find one or more leaders with sufficient reputation within the institution to light the educational fire to initiate such a program. It probably would be best to start small, with one interprofessional course, and then expand as the program identifies more faculty and students who become advocates. It is also necessary that the administrative hierarchy at the academic health center strongly support, and even take a leadership or advocacy position, to ensure both official and financial support for the endeavor. Some institutions have begun interdisciplinary efforts within a given field, such as medicine or nursing, and this may then provide the nexus for expansion as students and faculty become familiar with the context of such education.

Identifying Necessary Resources

Resources (space, faculty time, clinical sites, etc.) should be identified early in the process so that the program can expand as the concept grows and becomes accepted (Curley et al. 1998; Felten et al. 1997).

ISSUES TO BE ADDRESSED

In conceiving and developing a program in interprofessional education, a variety of factors must be addressed to ensure success. Strategies to deal with what Baldwin (1996) calls the challenges of interprofessional education must be developed. Some of these challenges are discussed below.

Inexperience

Faculty accustomed to instructing within their discipline, and largely by lecture, will be challenged by interprofessional education: The students vary from those they have had in the past, and the demand for small-group instruction calls for different skills. To address this issue, it is essential that a group of educational professionals and/or faculty well versed in these techniques be utilized in faculty development workshops, seminars, and individualized instruction. Educators must become knowledgeable about the characteristics of other health professional curricula and exchange traditional lecturing skills for those that facilitate small-group interaction.

An office of professional education is a useful institutional entity for processing these methods and enhancing faculty learning. This office would employ educational professionals conversant with the literature, knowledgeable about instruction and learning methods, familiar with initiating new endeavors in the curriculum, and generally helpful to faculty as the latter attempt to adapt to the somewhat new imperatives in interprofessional education. The office can also be useful in collaborating on design, implementation, and analysis of research conducted on the value of interprofessional education as well as providing the more usual assistance in student performance evaluation.

Student Differences

Students from the various health professions will vary widely in age, prior life experiences, professional expectations, maturity, and attitudes. These are not impenetrable barriers, as our experience at Colorado has shown. However, faculty and students must be made aware of these differences, as should those planning the learning experiences. One illustration of the potential disparities is a small group in our recent interprofessional ethics course. Students include a twenty-two-year-old medical student who has gone straight through her education, two graduate engineers, a nursing doctoral candidate with considerable clinical experience, several somewhat younger physical therapy students, and an older male physician assistant student who, before embarking on his current professional education, had had agricultural experiences and several other careers. Despite this broad range, the small group was able to integrate everyone's opinions, knowledge, and experiences into their discussions. When varying knowledge or experience caused students to differ on questions of fact, a quick explanation set the stage for continued dialogue.

There were three facilitators, also diverse in background: a medical resident, a full-time ethics faculty member with a degree in English and accomplishments in using the humanities in education, and myself. We also varied widely in age. Nevertheless, the group functioned harmoniously, engaged in scholarly discussion, and produced oral and written reports. Their performance indicates that this disparate group appears to have succeeded in meeting the objectives of the course.

Physical and Scheduling Difficulties

Lack of adequate space for the newer types of education and for clinical encounters of the teamwork type, added to the fact that separate professional schools tend to cling to their own unique schedules, creates potential barriers to success. Strong administrative support, essential to identifying existing space and developing new space, can diminish that barrier and overcome the daunting issue of differing schedules. For the latter, one may discover that an hour is not the same from school to school, that the year is divided into different academic terms (semesters, trimesters, etc.), and that vacations or breaks may vary. It takes a strong central administrative presence and a strong institutional ethos to overcome these disparities to either ensure uniform schedules or to accommodate the differences by creatively scheduling the interprofessional course. In our own experience, we offered one course prior to commencing any of the individual professional curricula, and overcame participants' disparate break schedules by recording the one missed encounter.

Paucity of Role Models

The typical academic health center often lacks sufficient role models to both instruct and inspire students in the correct attitudes and skills. This can lead to a do-as-I-say, not-as-I-do kind of skepticism on the part of students in the interprofessional educational program. One solution to this problem is to find appropriate settings within the community and establish appropriate teams in those settings from the academic community. The alternative to this strategy is the far less adequate approach of emphasizing to the students that we are in a changing culture, and they will be the pioneers.

Lack of Leadership

This is a complex issue ranging from total advocacy and commitment to active opposition by those in the most influential administrative positions. In addition, many faculty groups characteristically resist change. The only solutions are either to convince leaders of the validity of the interprofessional approach or change the key leaders to those who embrace and are willing to champion appropriate change. These are difficult choices, but the imperatives of today's environment, which mandate multiple changes in attitude and behavior in academic health centers, demand that difficult choices be made. Failure to do so can result in stagnation and, as some academic health centers have discovered, failure of the enterprise.

Inappropriate Reward and Activity Structure

One issue that must be addressed at the outset is a disparity between the demands for faculty participation in interprofessional education and faculty perception of the academic, financial, and reputational rewards that accompany their involvement. Many institutions so strongly stress the importance of research and clinical activity to promotions and pay that teaching seems to be only a side issue. That culture must be changed if faculty are to devote the enthusiastic effort they are capable of giving to interprofessional education. The use of varying criteria for promotion, tenure, and salary that include legitimate teaching and innovation in education can encourage faculty to participate. Some innovative approaches to this problem have been outlined by Mennin and Kalishman (1998).

BENEFITS TO THE ACADEMIC HEALTH CENTER

Why should an academic health center want to participate in this new educational endeavor? Apart from the fact that it is the correct educational direction, given the current clinical milieu their students will enter, there are other tangible and intangible advantages to the academic health center. Some of these follow.

Efficiency of Education

In the long run, greater efficiency will be achieved across the many professions represented on a given campus. For example, if all health professions students are taught basic sciences together, the academic health centers' individual schools, which currently duplicate educational efforts, will conserve considerable faculty time and dollars. Like many changes, this one will initially detract from efficiency until faculty set aside time for planning, for learning the new techniques involved in interprofessional education, and for actually participating. But as the process matures, greater effort by fewer faculty will serve larger numbers of students.

Appreciation of Other Professions

Those who participate in interprofessional educational encounters learn to appreciate other disciplines. In today's clinical arena, one cannot stress enough the necessity for greater regard and respect for disciplines other than one's own. We need to rise above the petty territoriality and turf issues that plague many academic health centers—and the professions at large—so that we deliver the best possible care to our patients. It is encouraging to note that one study suggests that such tolerance and appreciation do result from an interprofessional educational setting (Hayward et al. 1996). Energy, resources, and emotions are spent foolishly protecting—or thinking that we protect—our discipline from perceived incursions from other professions. We should spend that energy, emotion, and those resources on teamwork and learning how we can all cooperate to benefit the patient primarily, and to make our professional activities both more efficient and more satisfying.

Improvement of Community Relations

Interprofessional partnerships can also have the outstanding benefit of a better blending of community and academe. The town-gown issue has plagued our academic health centers long enough. Many have learned the benefits of closer ties with the community, and interprofessional education can further that cause. Along with the professional barriers that can be cast aside, the lay community will learn more about the academic health center, and such activities as advocacy and philanthropy may be enhanced.

Improvement of Interpersonal Relationships on Campus

Interprofessional education has the potential to create new alliances among diverse professional faculty, leading to interactions that might never have been conceived of in our monolithic structure. Ideas for new course work, research, or clinical care may grow from the unique contact that interprofessional education provides. In fact, collaborative, interprofessional research can be a tangible benefit to faculty who may not see other advantages to this type of effort.

Graduation of Better Students

I am convinced that students who are educated in an interprofessional program will have greater ability to work on a team in a medical practice, in academe, in public health, or in other health-related endeavors, and will demonstrate greater respect for and knowledge of their colleagues in other disciplines. We have seen a beginning of this process on our campus as students report that they never knew the scope and possibilities of their colleagues' professional skills in disciplines other than their own. Students also say that they have a greater respect for the educational rigor of other curricula, having assumed theirs was the only rigorous regimen. Many express a much better understanding of professional interaction with others when they reach their clinical arenas.

A FINAL WORD

Interprofessional education is the right thing to do at the right time in the history of academe, education, research, and clinical care. We need to approach this activity as rigorously as we do the other parts of our academic effort. Careful planning, design, and implementation must be accompanied by an effort to investigate the efficacy of this educational method, for both learning and practice. Integration into clinical practice appears essential given the current need for integrated care at reasonable cost. The potential efficiencies of teamwork, in contrast to the monolithic, fragmented care of the past, argues for both its implementation in practice and for study of its effectiveness.

Such a combination of potential advances in education, research, and clinical practice should be attractive to faculty who prize this triad as their mission. Interprofessional education presents abounding opportunities to advance our knowledge, to provide better care, and to create a better learning environment for our students.

WORK CITED

Baldwin, D.C. 1994. *The Role of Interdisciplinary Education and Teamwork in Primary Care and Health Reform.* Washington: U.S. Department of Health and Human Services.

Baldwin, D.C. 1996. Some historical notes on interdisciplinary and interprofessional education and practice in health care in the USA. *Journal of Interprofessional Care* 10:173–87.

_____. 1998. The case for interdisciplinary education. In *Mission Management: A New Synthesis,* Vol. 1. Washington: Association of Academic Health Centers.

Blue, A.V., C.H. Griffith, III, T.D. Stratton, L.T. Degnore, S.A. Haist, and R.W. Schwartz. 1998. Evaluation of students' learning in interdisciplinary medicine-surgery clerkship. *Academic Medicine* 73:806–08.

Browne, B., C. Carpenter, C. Cooledge, G. Drover, J. Ericksen, D. Fielding, D. Hill, J. Johnston, S. Segal, J. Silver, and V. Sweeney. 1995. Bridging the professions: An integrated and interdisciplinary approach to teaching health care ethics. *Academic Medicine* 70:1002–05.

Buckle, J.M., P. Myirski, and M. Myers. 1999. A medical center's successful care management program. *Drug Benefit Trends* 11:40, 43–44, 47–48.

Bulger, R.J. and R.E. Bulger. 1990. Obstacles to collegiality in the academic health center. *Bulletin of the New York Academy of Sciences* 68:303–07.

Caplan, P., D. Lefkowitz, and L. Spector. 1992. Health care consortia: A mechanism for increasing access for the medically indigent. *Henry Ford Hospital Medical Journal* 40:50–55.

COGME (Council on Graduate Medical Education). 1997. *Preparing Learners for Practice in a Managed Care Environment.* Washington: U.S. Department of Health and Human Services.

Commission on Medical Education. 1992. *Medical Education in Transition: The Sciences of Medical Practice.* Princeton: Robert Wood Johnson Foundation.

Curley, C., J.E. McEachern, and T. Speroff. 1998. A firm trial of interdisciplinary rounds on the inpatient medical wards: An intervention designed using continuous quality improvement. *Medical Care* 36:AS 4–12.

DePoy, E., C. Wood, and M. Miller. 1997. Educating rural allied health professionals: An interdisciplinary effort. *Journal of Allied Health* 26:127–32.

Egan, C., and D. Jewler. 1997. The impact of managed oncology care: Integration or disintegration? *Oncology Issues* 12:22–27.

Fagin, C.M. 1992. Collaboration between nurses and physicians, no longer a choice. *Academic Medicine* 66:295–303.

Felten, S., N. Cady, M.H. Metzler, and S. Burton. 1997. Implementation of collaborative practice through interdisciplinary rounds on a general surgery service. *Nursing Case Management* 2:122–26.

Goldberg, A.I. 1995. Pediatric home health: The need for physician education. *Pediatrics* 95:928–30.

Gordon, J.I., and D.M. Kipnis. 1999. Creating the future rather than simply reacting to it. *Pharos* 62:9–12.

Gordon, P.R., L. Carlson, A. Chessman, M.L. Kundrat, P.S. Morahan, and L.A. Headrick. 1996. A multisite collaborative for the development of interdisciplinary education in continuous improvement for health professions students. *Academic Medicine* 71:973–78.

Hayward, K.S, L.T. Powell, and J. McRoberts. 1996. Changes in student perceptions of interdisciplinary practice in the rural setting. *Journal of Allied Health* 25:315–27.

Hensel, W.A., D.D. Smith, D.R. Barry, and R. Foreman. 1996. Changes in medical education: The community perspective. *Academic Medicine* 71:441–46.

Kent, H. 1997. Medical, health-science students bring different perspectives to interdisciplinary ethics course. *Canadian Medical Association Journal* 156:1317–18.

Lavoie, S.R., and L.G. Kaplowitz. 1996. Family centered HIV/AIDS care. *The AIDS Reader* 6:117–21, 137.

Mennin, S.P., and S. Kalishman. 1998. Issues and strategies for reform in medical education: Lessons from eight medical schools. *Academic Medicine* 73:supplement, September.

O'Neil, E.H. 1993. *Health Professions Education for the Future: Schools in Service to the Nation.* San Francisco: Pew Health Professions Commission.

Ray, M.D. 1998. Shared borders: Achieving the goals of interdisciplinary education. *American Journal of Health-System Pharmacy* 55:1369–74.

Reitan, J.F. 1996. Current concepts in managing cancer pain. *Drug Benefit Trends.* 37:41, 45–48.

Sataloff, R.T. 1997. Treating common disorders of the voice. *Hospital Medicine* 33:47–48, 53–54, 56, 59–60.

———. 1998. Interdisciplinary opportunities for creativity in medicine. *Ear, Nose and Throat Journal* 77:530–33.

Shuster, A.L. and R.C. Reynolds. 1998. Medical education: Can we do better? *Academic Medicine* 73:Sv-Si.

Simon, S.R., R.J.D. Pan, A.M. Sullivan, N. Clark-Chiarelli, M.T. Connelly, A.S. Peters, J.D. Singer, T.S. Invi, and S.D. Block. 1999. Views of managed care. *New England Journal of Medicine* 340:928–36.

Singleton, J.K., and C. Green-Hernandez. 1998. Interdisciplinary education and practice. Has its time come? *Journal of Nurse Midwifery* 43:3–7.

Stair, J. 1998. Understanding the challenges for hospice: Fundamental for the future. *Oncology Issues* 13:22–25.

Wartmann, S.A., A.K. Davis, M.E.H. Wilson, N.B. Kahn, and R.H. Kahn. 1998. Emerging lessons of the Interdisciplinary Generalist Curriculum (IGC) Project. *Academic Medicine* 73:935–42.

EAST CAROLINA UNIVERSITY

3
Retooling to Meet the Needs of a Changing Health Care System

Maria C. Clay, PhD; Doyle M. Cummings, PharmD, FCP, FCCP, Chris Mansfield, PhD, and James A. Hallock, MD

I t is no longer news to anyone that the health care delivery system, changing at an alarming rate, is producing profound changes even in smaller communities. These forces will continue to drive the reorganization of the health care delivery system, forcing it to provide cost-effective, efficient care for what will be a population of covered lives via some combination of risk-sharing capitation and discounted fee for service. As a result, the health care workplace will demand new professional skills, new configurations of staff, and new numbers of practitioners.

EXTERNAL FORCES SHAPE THE NEED
FOR INTERDISCIPLINARY EDUCATION

We believe that this reorganization will demand that health professionals collaborate in an interdisciplinary fashion to plan and deliver cost-efficient care. Although we have all practiced in a multidisciplinary fashion, referring patients to providers when appropriate, we talk here about a patient care plan that is the product of the interdisciplinary interaction of different health professionals working as a team. The emphasis in this paper, therefore, is on collaboration. For example, the diabetic patient in this new capitated health delivery system is going to be managed by the right health professional at the right time, using a care plan that has been forged by this collaborative process.

The implications for health professions education are clear. We need to train learners who are not only competent in their own disciplines but also able to work side by side with other health professionals to provide quality health care at a price our nation can afford.

Training health professionals to practice in a collaborative fashion in an evolving health care system is a major challenge. Unfortunately, many institutions of higher education are unprepared to effect the significant restructuring necessary for interdisciplinary training, despite the call by Pew Commission reports to provide a broader set of system, organizational, and population skills to students. Classroom education is important, but practical models of collaboration are also necessary to infuse a critical sense of reality into the learning process.

Another important force in the context of this rapidly changing health care delivery system is a shift in focus from providers of care to outcomes of care. Many observers no longer support an early assumption that improving the health of a population was simply a function of the number and types of providers. Rather, there is a growing view that we have a sufficient health care workforce, albeit inadequately distributed, and that investing more tax dollars in health care education is unnecessary. Instead, insurers are looking at the outcomes of care for populations of patients and for specific diseases with a goal of providing the highest quality of care for the least cost. Decisions regarding the proper mix of providers and the content of their work are being left up to the health care delivery system, which must operate within a specific budget and demonstrate good outcomes.

INTERDISCIPLINARY PRACTICE: A HISTORY OF SUCCESS

Early evidence suggests that interdisciplinary practice models can result in a variety of important outcomes (Bellin and Geiger 1970; Garfield et al. 1976; Beloff and Korper 1972; Chabot 1971; and Hocheiser et al. 1971). Specific benefits have included enhanced patient compliance and greater patient satisfaction; increased efficiency and reduced costs; reduction in broken appointments; and decreases in hospitalization, costs of care, and use of physicians. Studies have also found lower infant mortality rates, fewer hospitalizations, and fewer emergency room visits, as well as fewer visits for illness and more visits for health supervision. In addition, a number of inpatient models of care, including some in rehabilitation medicine, psychiatric medicine, nutritional support, and other disciplines, have a long history of utilizing a variety of health care professionals to develop collaborative care plans for hospitalized patients.

A Clarion Call

A few years ago, a Pew Commission report renewed its call for interprofessional collaboration and teams in patient care. Tresolini and the Pew Fetzer Task Force (1994) state the following:

> Recommendation 3: Require interdisciplinary competence in all health professionals. This competency is listed among [a longer list of] the 21 [competencies deemed necessary for health professionals], but is so essential for the future that it is emphasized here. Today's best integrated health delivery systems are evolving toward a model of care in which interdisciplinary teams of providers manage the care of the sickest patients. This model, which involves physicians, nurses, and allied professionals, is proving its worth with both acutely and chronically ill patients. Resources are used in the most timely and efficient way; mistakes or duplication of services is avoided; and the expertise and instincts of a number of trained health practitioners are brought to bear in an environment that values brainstorming, consultation, and collaboration. This is not a value that has been inculcated in health professional training programs of the past. Medical and professional schools should fundamentally reassess their curricula to ensure that their programs embody and apply an interdisciplinary vision. Specifically,
> - Care delivery systems should work with local educational programs to describe and demonstrate how interdisciplinary skills are being incorporated into practice.
> - Schools and faculties should target 25 percent of their current educational offerings that could more efficiently and effectively be offered in interdisciplinary settings.
> - Students should seek their own opportunities to study or work in environments that expose them to interdisciplinary care as early as possible.

Discussing "work in interdisciplinary teams," the report states,

> Researchers are beginning to confirm what many caregivers have suspected intuitively for a long time: the coordinated efforts of practitioners from many disciplines provide the best outcomes for the sickest patients. The future of medicine will call on all health professions—doctors, dentists, nurses, pharmacists, allied professionals, and public health and social workers,—to work together in more focused ways. Comprehensive care of individuals and populations requires a wide range of knowledge and skills and involves a variety of delivery settings. To assure effective and efficient coordination of care, health professionals must work interdependently in carrying out their roles and responsibilities, conveying mutual respect, trust, support and appreciation of each discipline's unique contributions to health care.

Specific recommendations to address interdisciplinary competency include the following:

> - Introduce students to the spectrum of health professionals and their respective and

complementary roles in health care delivery.
- Incorporate planned interdisciplinary experiences in the curriculum, e.g., interdisciplinary courses, seminars, clinical experiences, research projects.
- Provide structured experiences in case management and coordination.
- Actively model effective interdisciplinary collaboration and team integration in teaching, research, and clinical practice.

In addition, the consensus statement of the National League for Nursing's Interdisciplinary Health Education Panel calls for a strong link between education and practice components that can prepare health professionals for interprofessional collaboration (Walker et al. 1993).

Role of Funders

The resurgence of interest in interdisciplinary practice models can also be linked to the forward-minded thinking of leaders in key funding agencies. These have included, among others, the Pew Charitable Trust, which funded the Pew Health Commission; the U.S. Bureau of Health Professions, which funds an interdisciplinary rural health training program; the Area Health Education Centers Program; and The Robert Wood Johnson Foundation, which has supported a series of initiatives including the Generalist Physicians Initiative and the Partnerships for Training programs.

The Need for Leadership

Producing such a major shift in the direction of health professions education also requires leadership. Visionary leaders who see the value of interdisciplinary training and practice are working in selected universities and health systems to bring about needed change. This leadership may exist in the administrative staff or flow from a handful of faculty and staff who see the future and are willing to invest the effort to shape a process of change.

DEVELOPMENT OF A COMMUNITY-BASED MODEL

At East Carolina University (ECU), the vice chancellor for health sciences and key faculty have provided the impetus for an interdisciplinary model. Such leadership support engenders the buy-in of faculty and key stakeholders, which encourages institutional change.

ECU is situated in eastern North Carolina, a vast rural medically underserved area. Many of the counties in this region have alarming health statistics, including morbidity and mortality rates that exceed state and national averages.

It is understandable that for the ECU Division of Health Sciences (Schools of Medicine, Nursing, and Allied Health) and the Eastern Area Health Education Center (EAHEC), the prime mission is service to the region with the expectation that it will ultimately improve health outcomes. The strong emphasis on service to the people of eastern North Carolina permeates many of the programs and degrees at the university. It has also led to interdisciplinary programs with strong community components and goals that go well beyond training health care students in interdisciplinary principles and practices.

Unlike more traditional approaches to interdisciplinary education, ECU did not begin by developing an interdisciplinary campus course or creating interdisciplinary credit programs. Instead, the interdisciplinary education centered on experiences in the rural settings where collaboration would ultimately take place.

The community-based education model has many advantages, as follows:

1. The model strengthens the student's confidence in interdisciplinary collaboration. Students see such collaboration in health care delivery first-hand and experience for themselves the efficacy of providing coordinated care to patients. It is at this juncture, when patients are better served through collaborative interdisciplinary care, that students learn the most.

2. Community-based interdisciplinary education allows local practitioners/preceptors to offer interdisciplinary education and change practice patterns in their communities simultaneously. We all know that role modeling is critical in health care education; it is even more so in interdisciplinary education. To be effective interdisciplinary role models, community preceptors must practice in more collaborative ways. For this reason, community-based programs place a heavy emphasis on preceptor-development programs. These programs provide a setting in which preceptors from a variety of disciplines learn from one another, acquire skills together, get to know one another personally and professionally, and begin dialogues that ultimately lead to practice changes. Once forged, these relationships and changes in practice serve both learners and patients.

3. Community-based interdisciplinary programs have enabled university

faculty to interact more with community preceptors, leading to a better under-standing of the needs of both specific populations and local practitioners. With this information, university faculty can alter courses, advise students more accu-rately, and help communities promote health for the region.

4. Our rural community-based model has encouraged us to explore new technologies: teleconferencing between sites to link students to one another and to their university faculty; tele-meetings that enable community partners to have input in the decision-making process; and E-mail that links community sites to each other and to the university. These technological initiatives have opened new doors for curriculum delivery: for example, Web-based threaded discussions for case conferences; access to the health sciences library from afar; and access to the Internet. They have also encouraged community agencies to seek alternative methods for communicating among themselves.

5. Our rural community-based model has given rise to new decision-mak-ing models with lasting community effects. Advisory groups in the community, set up to aid in the design and oversight of community-based education, have matured into cross-agency health-planning groups. These groups, which involve local agency leadership as well as local citizens, are cognizant of the health prob-lems in their community. They are able to set priorities for filling these needs and then seek the assistance of students as well as the resources of the university to help address the problems. In this way, the health-planning groups have gone far beyond merely educating students to seek ways to deliver more effective health care. The relationship between community agencies, the university, and EAHEC has matured significantly over time. As a result, university/EAHEC expertise has aided communities in obtaining much-needed funds, and community expertise has aided the academic health science center in planning new health initiatives for the region.

6. Using a rural community-based model for interdisciplinary education has necessitated new evaluation strategies. Assessment of student learning is only one piece of the evaluation picture. Evaluation strategies need to be put into place to capture changes in the community's health outcomes as a result of having students in town and the university having a presence in the community. Assessment rela-tive to changing practice patterns as a result of community-preceptor collabora-tion and the evolving nature of community-university partnerships all become critical components of the evaluation strategies. Equally as important is the stu-dents' perception that interdisciplinary collaboration, rural career options, and ulti-mate employment in underserved areas have also become critical components of our evaluation.

Although not all ECU interdisciplinary programs are community based, most have a service component and seek the collaboration and inclusion of community partners in the delivery of education to students. We believe that the rural community focus of the interdisciplinary programs makes them unique and serves the needs of the student, the faculty, the community, and the people of eastern North Carolina.

The Interdisciplinary Rural Health Training Program

With institutional support and external funding from the Duke Endowment and the U.S. Bureau of Health Professions, the faculty and staff of the Interdisciplinary Rural Health Training Program have been privileged to establish an interdisciplinary training program in eastern North Carolina. The program, started in 1994, is designed around the principles articulated in the Pew Report; its vision is to leverage the opportunities provided by the concurrent community-based education of health science students from multiple disciplines.

The idea of providing a value-added curriculum that spans all disciplines without interfering with the discipline-specific training necessary for licensing and subsequent practice has been implemented. Students in ten different disciplines (table 1) from multiple universities and Area Health Education Center regions in North Carolina (figure 1) have collaborated to support this initiative.

Figure 1
Interdisciplinary Rural Health Training Program Sites, ECU/EAHEC

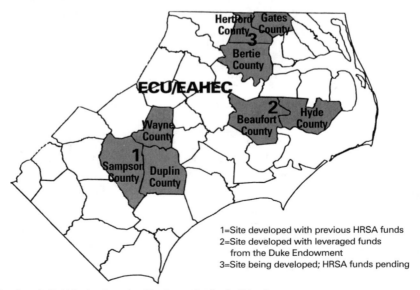

1=Site developed with previous HRSA funds
2=Site developed with leveraged funds
    from the Duke Endowment
3=Site being developed; HRSA funds pending

Map from Center for Health Services Research and Development, East Carolina University

Table 1
Partners in the Interdisciplinary Rural Health Training Program

Discipline	University	AHEC Region	Rural County
Health education	East Carolina University	Eastern	Beaufort
Medicine	Duke University	Southern Regional	Duplin
Nurse practitioner	Campbell University	Coastal	Hyde
Nursing	UNC-Greensboro		Bertie
Nutrition	UNC-Chapel Hill		Hertford
Occupational therapy	UNC-Wilmington		Gates
Pharmacy	NC Central		
Physical therapy	NC A & T		
Physician assistant			
Social work			

The long-term goal of this program is to create a positive environment for health care delivery in rural eastern North Carolina by improving the recruitment and retention of health care professionals trained in effective interdisciplinary care.

The curriculum. By design, the value-added curricula are being delivered and evaluated on site in three rural communities of fewer than 5,000 people each. Students who elect to take this training rotate at one of three medical school sites for a period of up to twelve months, depending upon other course work and electives in their disciplines.

This training is not required. Instead, faculty advisors recruit students to complete the required clerkship training in a rural community where a value-added curriculum is available. The core elements include activities to expose students in a structured way to other disciplines (e.g., cross-disciplinary training and team home visits), institute collaborative patient management through carefully planned interdisciplinary case conferences, and encourage rural practice through a series of team community experiences. Students are also encouraged to work together on community projects that have been identified by local citizens. For example, students collaborated to provide a free health fair for employees of a local food-processing plant. Here, health information was provided on HIV/AIDS and the prevention of other sexually transmitted diseases, prenatal care to minimize infant mortality, and chronic disease management. In addition, employees were screened for hypertension and tuberculosis.

The curriculum is designed so that the local community serves as a full partner. Students review their learning with a team of local preceptors and also the broader community. Students play an active role in the governance of the program by attending Community Advisory Meetings, complete learning contracts reviewed by community preceptors, and plan case conferences under the tutelage and guidance of community preceptors.

Preceptor development. Early in the project, program personnel realized that community preceptors were not comfortable in their roles as either discipline-specific preceptors or teachers in an interdisciplinary curriculum. Interviews with preceptors and written evaluations from students confirmed both the lack of comfort and the perceived lack of skills on the part of the community preceptors.

As a result, program personnel designed a preceptor development program with three principal goals: to make preceptors more comfortable with the interdisciplinary curriculum; to help preceptors become more comfortable with their roles as teachers and evaluators; and to make the preceptors more comfortable with one another. Twelve community preceptors, representing the six disciplines initially affiliated with the project, attended four 3-hour preceptor development sessions.

The instructional model was an adult education experiential model in which participants learn their roles, become acquainted with the interdisciplinary curriculum, and feel more comfortable as preceptors by actually participating in various components of the interdisciplinary curriculum. The initial training program consisted of sessions dealing with

- Giving effective feedback;
- Conducting an interdisciplinary case conference;
- Guiding students in conducting an interdisciplinary case conference (pre- and post-conference counseling); and
- Negotiating cross-training expectations.

The first program was held at one site, then repeated the next evening for the participants at a second site. This deliberate effort to take the training to the people enabled us to model collaboration between the academic medical center and the community, enhance team building between preceptors on site, and experience components of the interdisciplinary program at locations where the students would ultimately be trained.

At the end of the semester following the preceptor training program, evaluations were conducted. Preceptors were once again interviewed, and written comments of the students were collected and analyzed. The combined data reveal that

- Preceptors felt more comfortable with their roles;
- Preceptors had a heightened sensitivity to the needs of other disciplines based on their participation in the case conference;
- Students felt that they had learned from other disciplines; and
- Preceptors felt more comfortable giving students feedback.

Since this initial training, all preceptors who participate in the interdisciplinary curriculum are provided preceptor development. If the numbers are large enough, group sessions are held. If turnover is low and only a few new preceptors are added to the program, a more individualized approach is taken. The aim of the training remains the same: to facilitate comfort with the interdisciplinary curriculum; to impart skills in teaching and evaluating; and to make the preceptor feel like a member of the interdisciplinary program linked with others in the community who also teach interdisciplinary students.

Most recently, an advanced preceptor development program has been developed to help local organizations that wish to convert their practice model to one involving interdisciplinary teams. A pilot program conducted with a local health department enabled the program planners to define a process in which topics would be selected and an evaluation scheme determined. It

> *We realize the need for a protocol for forging collaborative relationships in the local community.*

is our expectation that an advanced preceptor development program, collaboratively planned and conducted by academic health center personnel and local leaders, will facilitate the creation of organizations that can model the interdisciplinary principles we want our students to learn.

Housing. From its inception, the program provided housing for students to live together in the community. This enabled easy communication, provided a wealth of resource sharing, and fostered insights unavailable in other venues. The houses were also linked via computer to the university, the library, the Internet, and each other.

Curriculum modifications. Using a public health model as the basis for our curriculum development permits community needs to drive the learning of those students immersed in the community. And as new interdisciplinary teaching sites are added, curriculum modifications are made to meet the needs of both the site and the students who will ultimately rotate in that community.

The process is collaborative. For example, this past year an interdisciplinary committee of faculty and staff, with input from local preceptors, researched and designed a new, site-specific curriculum. It incorporates the core elements of the interdisciplinary program (case conferences, community site experiences, and cross-discipline visits). However, the new curriculum also features a classroom lecture, a series of readings, and faculty-advising delivered on campus that broaden exposure to the concept of interdisciplinary education. Moreover, the new curriculum focuses interdisciplinary training around the disease state, diabetes mellitus. This disease was selected because of its striking prevalence among adults in the region (approximately 8 to 10% vs 4.5% prevalence among adults statewide) and because the profound health consequences of the disease require care by multiple health care providers. Teaching strategies to engage students in a process of collaborative learning and provide care for patients with diabetes mellitus were designed and are being delivered.

Governance. The program is governed by an Executive Council with representation from faculty in each discipline, community-based representatives, program administrators, program consultants, and an academic fellow. This council meets quarterly to track progress of the program, plan for student rotations, discuss and implement programmatic changes, and plan for program expansion.

Evaluation. From the program's inception, evaluation has been contracted to an evaluator outside the project team. The program directors, program coordinator, and fellow delineate specific evaluation tasks (e.g., development of an evaluation protocol and corresponding instruments, collection/analysis of data, and preparation of a completed report). A nonprogram faculty member, however, has performed the actual evaluation. This strategy has enabled program planners to assess student learning and administrative issues, and to feel confident that the evaluation is as objective as possible.

Preliminary results indicate that the service-learning and interdisciplinary components of the program have markedly enhanced student learning. The interdisciplinary program has also strengthened the infrastructure and commitment of the university for decentralized education. Thus, the university has expanded community services that include changes in the staff mix and institutional goals, the development of team-based care paths, and more positive attitudes of providers regarding interdisciplinary-service learning.

Preliminary assessment of the program has also taught us some valuable lessons. We are well aware of the importance of site-selection to the success of the program and the need for specific criteria for making the site selections.

We also realize the need for a protocol for forging collaborative relationships in the local community. Success cannot come without (1) a faculty/preceptor-training program that spans multiple disciplines, and (2) a process that generates community-sensitive projects and research. Many of the lessons learned have been presented at both state and national meetings.

Our experiences have also taught us that health professions students are socialized into their respective disciplines as a result of the structure of their discipline-specific curriculum. This situation may limit cross-disciplinary interaction unless specific interventions are made.

Research is currently underway to look at outcomes associated with this rural-based interdisciplinary process relative to more traditional educational programs. Our initial experience of more than 500 student months has been very positive in terms of both student and community outcomes. But a widespread expansion of this approach will require a new model of collaborative practice, a process for refining and customizing curriculum to specific sites, community preceptors who can teach and model these concepts, as well as a well-oiled system of coordination.

Changing the institution. As a result of this project and related work, the vice chancellor for health sciences named a Task Force on Interdisciplinary Health Sciences Education chaired by the codirectors of this project. This task force completed a major faculty-development colloquium in the spring of 1998. Denise Holmes, JD, MPH, director of the Center for Interdisciplinary, Community-Based Learning at the Association for Academic Health Centers, was keynote speaker.

The task force has since been constituted as a standing committee of the ECU Division of Health Sciences. In addition, the vice chancellor is establishing an Office of Interdisciplinary Health Sciences Education at the divisional level; it will be directed by the codirectors of the project, with faculty and staff appointed to the office from multiple interdisciplinary initiatives across the Division of Health Sciences.

The Tillery Project

Tillery, North Carolina, is an isolated rural community of 1,500 people, predominantly older African Americans who were resettled there by a Federal program in the Franklin D. Roosevelt Administration. They were without local medical care until about twelve years ago; at that point, a faculty member from East Carolina University School of Medicine (ECUSM) began visiting and later began bringing medical students to the community to provide limited medical care. The community became engaged and turned an old farm building into a usable clinic with donated equipment and supplies. Students began coming for regular monthly clinics.

About four years ago, with funding from the Federal Learn and Serve program, student involvement with the community was expanded. The disciplines involved included medicine, physical therapy, speech and audiology, nutrition, nursing, environmental science, recreation and leisure studies, occupational therapy, and community health education.

Students now collaboratively provide care in the local community. This service is an elective for some students and required for others. Approximately 200 students have participated thus far. The core of the project remains the health clinic, which provides services including basic health screening; health education; treatment of some acute illnesses such as upper respiratory infection and vaginal infection; and management of uncomplicated chronic diseases. Community volunteers provide administrative services (e.g., filing records, scheduling appointments, and arranging for local transportation).

Students have also collaborated on a comprehensive needs assessment. As a result, students and community members teamed up to construct a walking trail for senior citizens and a basketball court for youth. These amenities have been valuable in efforts to prevent and treat diseases such as diabetes mellitus, which is associated with obesity and physical inactivity. Indeed, the entire project has been invaluable because of the collaboration of various disciplines.

Partnerships for Training

An innovative joint project between East Carolina University and Duke University, Partnerships for Training, has been developed with funding from The Robert Wood Johnson Foundation. It is designed to help ease the shortage of primary health care providers in rural eastern North Carolina by allowing area residents to train as primary care practitioners without attending a traditional, campus-based education program. The residents can train as nurse practitioners (NP), physician assistants (PA), or certified nurse midwives (CNM) on a part-time basis, learning both at home and in their communities. This approach allows students to continue with their current lifestyle and work while taking the program.

The program has established its course sequence, determined shared credit hours, prepared cross-institutional course listings, and initiated cross-institutional faculty appointments. After two planning years, forty-one students (31 NP, 9 PA, and 1 CNM) signed up for the initial year, which started in the fall of 1998. As of this writing, fifty-one new students are anticipated in year two. Course work includes the use of computers, interactive video, hands-on training, and other innovative teaching methods.

Partners in this project are:
- Academy of Physician Assistants, North Carolina Chapter
- Carteret General Hospital, Morehead City
- Duke University, Durham
- East Carolina University, Greenville
- Eastern Area Health Education Center, Greenville
- Fayetteville Area Health Education Center, Fayetteville
- Martin General Hospital, Williamston
- North Carolina Nurses Association, Nurse Practitioner Council
- Sampson County Memorial Hospital, Clinton
- Southeastern Regional Medical Center, Lumberton
- North Carolina Area Health Education Center Program

- North Carolina Department of Human Resources, Office of Rural Health and Resource Development
- University of North Carolina at Pembroke/Fayetteville State University

In addition, the recruitment of associate degree and diploma nurses from the state's minority institutions is being encouraged.

Because primary care practitioners share some core competencies that allow them to help a variety of patient populations with a broad range of health concerns, this program allows for interdisciplinary education through common courses taught across the disciplines.

Interdisciplinary courses developed thus far include health promotion/disease prevention, physiology/pathophysiology, clinical pharmacology, health assessment/diagnostic reasoning, issues in health care organization, interdisciplinary roles seminar, informatics, research methods, and foundations of advanced practice.

The first year of instruction is delivered primarily via computer. Course assignments, communications with faculty and with fellow students in small group projects, and video and audio classes are also delivered through distance-based resources. Some course work is also provided face-to-face at local hospitals, clinics, and/or community colleges. Students are taught jointly by faculty from both East Carolina University and Duke University.

After the first year of study, students are placed in community settings with local preceptors, who come from the partners, usually in conjunction with students from other disciplines as they learn to provide primary care in local communities. Many students are also included in the Interdisciplinary Rural Health Training Program.

In general, this project's many strengths include a shared commitment to increase access to health care for underserved populations; strong, creative leadership; an integrated online university of resources, passionate local partners, motivated students, and an excellent academic team.

THE DEVELOPMENT OF CAMPUS-BASED COURSES

The PenPAL Project

The Pitt, Edgecombe, Nash Public Academic Liaison Project (PenPAL) is a partnership between East Carolina University and the mental health agencies in three eastern North Carolina counties. For the university, it involves a shared curriculum ("Interdisciplinary Practice—Services for Children with Serious Emotional Disorders and Their Families") for students in the Department of Psychology, the Department of Child Development and Family Relations,

School of Social Work, and School of Nursing. The course, which is an elective, is designed to prepare students in these four disciplines to participate in holistic interdisciplinary team practice in a variety of settings.

The course focus is on the theory and skills necessary for interdisciplinary, collaborative practice. It uses a system-of-care model that cuts across disciplines to provide mental health services for children with serious emotional disturbances and for their families. Students learn the significance of interdisciplinary collaboration in these cases as well as the strengths and weaknesses of an interdisciplinary model.

To date, a total of approximately eighty students from the four disciplines have completed course work and field training. Students are able to differentiate parallel practice, multidisciplinary practice, and interdisciplinary care. Students compare and contrast care planning by each discipline and learn to build interdisciplinary practice guidelines for collaborative care. Although predominantly campus based, teaching also includes discussion groups, role-playing, small-group exercises, panel discussions, and guest lectures by professionals from a variety of disciplines. This course, which has been well received, is linked to a series of subsequent field experiences in the counties mentioned in table 1, where students can learn to apply the concepts of interdisciplinary practice to meet the emotional needs of children in these rural counties.

The Interdisciplinary MPH Program

Eastern North Carolina suffers from serious, disproportionate, and persistent health problems and a documented shortage of personnel trained in public health. These are among the reasons both ECU faculty and the administration wanted to develop an interdisciplinary master of public health (MPH) program focused on rural community health issues from a population perspective, including the large segment of minority or underserved groups. At the same time, we felt that increased public health training would complement the traditional patient-specific focus of the existing medical care system.

It has been suggested that, in addition to the benefits accruing from medical diagnostic and therapeutic technologies, significant gains in health come from community-based, population-wide strategies designed to (1) change health behavior, and (2) tailor the health care system to focus on disease prevention and health promotion. The program concept was also consistent with our mission statement, which refers to improving the health of the citizens of eastern North Carolina.

From the outset, leadership in each of the relevant cognate disciplines (including medicine, nursing, allied health, health education, business, public administration, social work, sociology, economics, nutrition, and anthropology) pledged to collaborate to make the MPH program an interdisciplinary enterprise. Faculty from these multiple disciplines, departments, and schools came together to forge program plans, curriculum objectives, and teaching strategies.

Core knowledge areas have been shaped from multiple disciplines and include epidemiology, health services administration, social and behavioral sciences, environmental health sciences, research interpretation, and methodology. Moreover, professional concentrations, research, and service are directed toward solutions to health problems in rural communities. This exciting, interdisciplinary MPH degree tailored to the needs of the region is still in the planning stages.

SUMMARY

East Carolina University, in partnership with the AHEC system and local communities, has established a series of interdisciplinary initiatives designed to prepare graduates to practice in the health systems of tomorrow. These innovative initiatives have included both community-based and campus-based programs that have had an impact on learners in a wide variety of health science programs.

We believe the community-based model has particular utility for the training of health care practitioners and should be explored by most health science programs. The model has resulted in a series of important learner-specific and community-specific outcomes while fostering significant institutional change at ECU. Based on this initial success, an interdisciplinary MPH program is being developed with emphasis on the compelling health needs of the region.

Together, the campus-based and community-based programs have collectively positioned ECU and its partners as one of the leaders in bringing health sciences education to focus on interdisciplinary collaboration. This new approach is consistent with the recommendations of the 1994 report of the Pew Health Professions Commission.

WORK CITED

Bellin, S.S., and H.J. Geiger. 1970. Actual public acceptance of the neighborhood health center by the urban poor. *Journal of the American Medical Association* 214:2147–153.

Beloff, J.S. and M. Korper. 1972. The health team model and medical care utilization. *Journal of the American Medical Association* 219:359-66.

Chabot, A. 1971. Improved infant mortality rates in a population served by a comprehensive neighborhood health program. *Pediatrics* 47:989-94.

Garfield, S.R., M.F. Collen, R. Feldman, K. Soghikian, R. Richart, and J. Duncah. 1976. Evaluation of ambulatory medical care delivery system. *New England Journal of Medicine* 294:426-31.

Hocheiser, L.E., K. Woodward, and E. Charney. 1971. Effect of the neighborhood health center on the use of pediatric emergency departments in Rochester, NY. *New England Journal of Medicine* 285:148-52.

Tresolini, C.P. 1994. *Pew Fetzer Task Force: Health Professions Education and Relationship Centered Care.* San Francisco: Pew Health Professions Commission.

Walker, P.H., D. Baldwin, J.J. Fitzpatrick, and S. Ryan. 1998. Building community: Developing skills for interprofessional health professions education and relationship-centered care. *Journal of Allied Health* (27)3:174–75.

4

A Model for Partnerships Among Communities, Disciplines, and Institutions

Bruce A. Behringer, MPH, Wilsie S. Bishop, DPA, Joellen B. Edwards, PhD, and Ronald D. Franks, MD

In 1989, with the formation of a Division of Health Sciences (DHS), East Tennessee State University (ETSU) began a long journey. This journey significantly changed communities, faculty, and the way the institution viewed the process of the education of health professions students in medicine, nursing, and public and allied health.

Interdisciplinary education was not new nationally. However, it had no precedent at ETSU. Thus, the journey began with visionary leadership and developed into a search for new ways for communities, educators, and students to relate to each other and connect.

According to the deans of medicine, nursing, and public and allied health, whose colleges comprise the new division, the major key to the success of the quest for interdisciplinarity is found not so much in the specific definition of the word as it is in its values, concepts, and spirit (Edwards et al. 1998). At ETSU, this spirit manifests itself through respect among colleagues across disciplines who share successes and failures, work hard toward common goals, trust each other, support joint ventures, and sincerely applaud singular accomplishments.

Indeed, as much as interdisciplinarity is framed by differences, it is the realization and appreciation of team member similarities that form the basis for the partnerships: a complex of interpersonal interactions, philosophical convictions, and a realization that working together is "the right thing to do" (Stanton 1998). This paper describes the change process and outcomes of the model for partnerships that resulted at ETSU.

THE SETTING

East Tennessee State University is a comprehensive regional educational institution of 11,000 students located in the southern Appalachian Mountains. The university began as a normal school for the training of teachers in 1911 and has a strong sense of pride, place, and commitment to its rural heritage. Although the university draws students from all over the world, 80 percent come from within 75 miles of Johnson City, where ETSU is located. More than 50 percent are nontraditional students, and many are the first generation of their families to attend college. The primary service area of the university is the surrounding eight-county region, which is rural, mountainous, and significantly medically underserved.

Before DHS's establishment, each health science college operated as an independent unit within the university, interacting only superficially. DHS brought the colleges together under a vice president for health affairs who also serves as the dean of medicine. Its collective mission is to "provide comprehensive health programs within a community-based academic health center that will improve the health of the citizens of our rural region." Its comprehensive educational, practice, and research activities, along with national recognition for excellence in rural primary care, make it the flagship institution in the Tennessee Board of Regents system for the health sciences.

It was leaders from Mountain City, an unincorporated rural town of 1,800, who in 1989 first approached the deans of the three health sciences colleges for assistance in rebuilding their crumbling rural health care delivery system. Both medicine and nursing responded, starting the fledgling DHS on a continuing commitment to partner with underserved communities and the colleges within the new division. The ensuing partnership grew to merit the award of a W.K. Kellogg Foundation grant for Community Partnerships for Health Profession Education. More important, it changed the educational process and had a positive effect on the health of the rural partner communities.

A MODEL FOR INTERDISCIPLINARY, COMMUNITY-BASED HEALTH PROFESSIONS EDUCATION

Figure 1 displays an overview of the goals, strategies, and outcomes to date. Both internal and external forces shaped the model.

External Influences

National Direction. The Community Partnerships project was initiated by the

Figure 1
Building an Interdisciplinary Partnership for Rural Health

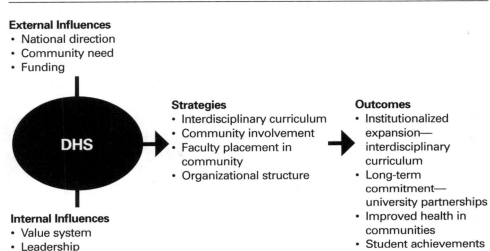

External Influences
- National direction
- Community need
- Funding

DHS

Strategies
- Interdisciplinary curriculum
- Community involvement
- Faculty placement in community
- Organizational structure

Outcomes
- Institutionalized expansion— interdisciplinary curriculum
- Long-term commitment— university partnerships
- Improved health in communities
- Student achievements

Internal Influences
- Value system
- Leadership
- Reward system

Kellogg Foundation in 1990, prior to the onslaught of other reports calling for national workforce changes, an emphasis on primary care, and increased interdisciplinary education. Over time, influential forces gathered in support of the implementation and sustainability of the project.

Increasingly, national attention was drawn to the excessive cost of health care in the United States. Issues of access, quality, and cost came to the forefront during the 1992 Presidential election, along with debate about the maldistribution between specialist and primary care providers. The Community Partnerships initiative, which focused on the accountability and responsibility of health professions education programs to address societal needs, was well positioned in the vision of state and Federal health care reformers. In the academic health center, where it was a controversial issue, it became a clarion call for supporters of change in health professions education and a dangerous enemy to opponents of many types of health systems, financing, and educational reform.

The report of Shugars et al. (1991) for the Pew Health Professions Commission added further legitimacy to the project's curriculum through its discussion of competencies for health care professionals in the twenty-first century. Several discipline-specific publications followed (Bondurant 1995; Ibrahin et al. 1995), reinforced by governmental reports (COGME 1992; Physician Payment Review Commission 1994). These were used by project leaders as evidence of the importance of the call for more primary care practitioners and adoption of interdisciplinary care teams.

Community Need. The local leaders who asked DHS for help in improving health care in their community expected that they, as taxpayers, would see the university rise to the occasion. In the first partner community, Mountain City, and also in the second partner, Rogersville, health status and the numbers of health care providers were at record lows. The percentage of physicians over 65 years of age was well above the national average. Registered nurses and allied health professionals were in short supply. The mortality rate from all causes was far higher than state and national rates. The use of preventive care was low, and many residents were medically uninsured. Both areas were chronically designated as health professions shortage areas, and their health care delivery systems were fragile.

The local citizenry was not disappointed as the leaders within the DHS responded. This early partnership to improve health gave the university and its partners a solid base for starting the new health professions education venture funded by the W.K. Kellogg Foundation.

Funding. The request for proposals from the W.K. Kellogg Foundation for a $6 million, five-year grant to form partnerships with communities to advance primary care and interdisciplinary health professions education had come at an opportune time. The three deans had already begun to work together and to form relationships with rural communities. The Kellogg grant awarded in 1991 helped frame the purpose, philosophy, and educational methods within the new division that have brought it a national reputation in primary care, rural health, community partnerships, and interdisciplinary innovation.

Internal Influences

Forces from within the university and the Division of Health Sciences helped shape the emerging model as well. As a new unit, the division was inventing its own history rather than overcoming barriers created in the past. The grant brought the newly formed division an opportunity for planned change. Its value system, the strengths of the leadership, and a willingness to reconsider traditional reward systems all contributed to the success of the emerging venture.

Value system. As members of a community-based academic health center, most faculty and administrators valued the center's community roots and connections. The College of Medicine had been formed as a university partnership forged with the Mountain Home Veterans Administration Medical Center through the Teague-Cranston Act in 1974. Medical residency programs were located throughout the region. Both nursing and public and allied health had long-standing community connections with agencies in the area. The step to partnering with rural communities became a natural extension of values already applied in the more urban Tri-Cities area of northeast Tennessee (Kingsport, Bristol, and Johnson City).

Leadership. The critical, early challenge to leadership was effectively communicating the vision of the project and encouraging faculty to become involved in the unfamiliar turf of interdisciplinary, community-based education. Though their styles differed, all three deans consistently supported the creation of a new division-wide norm of interdisciplinary understanding and commitment to meeting community needs. By adhering to their vision, they risked their professional standing among nonsupporters. But they formed a solid, united front. They set an example for others by staying actively involved in weekly meetings on campus and in communities an hour away from their schools.

> *[The division's] value system, the strengths of the leadership, and a willingness to reconsider traditional reward systems all contributed to the success of the emerging venture.*

As might be expected, even after receiving the Kellogg grant, faculty resistance and desire to maintain traditional approaches to teaching resulted in a sufficient level of conflict to require conflict resolution. The deans selected the high-risk approach of a two-day, off-campus "lock-in" retreat, moderated by professional conflict management consultants. The commitment to the program, gender issues, professional issues (especially between medicine and nursing), and strategies for implementation were all called into question. The tenacity of the deans in problem solving was the catalyst that allowed the faculty, upon their return to campus, to reconnect and recommit to the project.

The leadership of the project was, in short, visionary; they were willing to take risks, and were committed to communicating the vision for community-based, interdisciplinary education over and over again to constituents (Bishop 1998).

Although leadership of the project has changed, the current deans follow the same pattern of involvement and commitment. As founding deans moved on to new opportunities and others were recruited, search processes were heavily weighted toward finding people who would be compatible with the interdisciplinary, community-based model.

Reward system. Flexibility in the faculty reward system helped to promote visibility and openness to the project. Faculty who participated actively had the support of their deans. Workload time was assigned to the project faculty from each college. Travel to conferences and seminars was awarded to participants. The promotion and tenure system had enough latitude to value and reward community-based, interdisciplinary research. Service in the community, as well as service on campus, was recognized in faculty workloads and in the promotion and tenure processes.

GOALS OF THE PROJECT

The principles to be applied by recipients of the W.K. Kellogg Foundation Community Partnerships for Health Professions Education grants were simple. Grantees were to create a model for health professions education that (1) was focused on community-based primary care; (2) offered longitudinal experiences for participants; (3) provided interdisciplinary learning opportunities; and (4) gave communities a voice in the education of future health professionals.

The overarching project goals at ETSU became the creation of interdisciplinary, community-based education for medicine, nursing, and public and allied health students that would result in improved health for partner communities and more primary care providers prepared to care for underserved rural populations.

Strategies for Implementation

The strategies for accomplishing the goal of community-based, interdisciplinary health professions education began in 1990 and are still evolving today. Over time, the basic tenets have been reaffirmed countless times. The core methods included development of an interdisciplinary curriculum, establishment of a mechanism for a community voice in the training of health professionals, faculty integration into the partner communities, and creation of an organizational structure to oversee and guide the effort.

A full year, 1991, was spent in preparing the interdisciplinary curriculum. A team of faculty from the three participating colleges identified common educational objectives that could be learned by their students working together in the community. New interdisciplinary teaching teams were proposed. A two-year cohort of health professions students (a maximum of 25% of the students in the entering class of each college) was promised. The students selected to participate were first-year medical students, second-semester sophomore-level nursing students, and junior-level public or allied health students. They were to be representative of participating disciplines and linked to one of the partner communities over time. An interdisciplinary curriculum committee was organized to manage courses and identify needed resources.

Through persistent efforts, the barriers of disciplinary language, accreditation requirements, and bureaucratic rules were overcome. A core of thirteen interdisciplinary courses was approved through college and community curriculum committees, the university approval system, and the Tennessee Board of Regents. The first course was taught in July 1992. Each course is community based, with interdisciplinary faculty teams and student cohorts (Goodrow et al. 1996; Virgin et al. 1996, 1997; Olive et al. 1998). The courses are taught using experiential learning methods and are operationalized in the context of each unique partner community.

In 1996, curricular evaluation based upon outcome data from the first four years resulted in streamlining the course offerings from thirteen to nine and integrating the curriculum more deeply with the traditional offerings of each college. The nine courses are as follows:

Rural and Community Health (four courses offered in a progressive longitudinal sequence)
>Semester 1: Rural and Community Health Systems
>Semester 2: Strategies for Change
>Semester 3: Health Concerns and Needs of Rural Residents
>Semester 4: Community Health Project

Health Assessment (three courses)
>Semester 2: Health Assessment Examination I
>Semester 3: Health Assessment Examination II for Special Populations
>Semester 4: Patient/Client Assessment and Care Conference

Introduction to Rural Health (one course)
Communication Skills for Health Professionals (one course)

Because each college schedules its traditional courses independently, and students participating in the new program were also involved in campus requirements, logistics became a primary challenge. The colleges elected different methods to create opportunities for student involvement. Nursing elected to teach the majority of the bachelor's program in the rural communities, and encouraged students to live on site for an immersion experience. Medicine altered campus schedules in basic science courses significantly. Public health made course substitutions for specific undergraduate majors. The key to success was the colleges all setting aside one day each week as a "rural primary care track" day in both communities. A commitment was made (and is still honored) that participating students and faculty would be available on that day for rural, interdisciplinary, community-based activities.

The same course schedules are implemented in each of the partner communities. Distance from the university was overcome by providing cars for student travel to the sites; given the mountainous terrain, faculty opted for flexibility when winter weather interfered with travel. Linkages to library resources were formed electronically, and a fax and courier service assisted faculty and students on site.

The students who have entered the program over the years are often from a rural background and interested in primary care as a professional career option (Behringer et al. 1996). Pertinent student demographics are as follows:

- 84% were from rural communities (including the Tri-Cities area).
- 87% were from the Appalachian region (including Tennessee, Virginia, and North Carolina).
- 15% were recruited from out of state.
- 25.5 years was the average age at entry.

Community Involvement

The partner communities are deeply involved in the education of health professions students. Community curriculum committees were formed early in the process as part of the Community Advisory Boards. The role of these committees is not to dictate the professional aspects of the curriculum. Instead, their job is to work with faculty to make the health needs of the community known, identify resources for student learning, acquaint the students with the unique culture of the region, and make the community connections that will open doors for students and faculty in the rural area.

One key innovation introduced by viewing the entire community as a partner is the development of academic community health systems. This concept permitted an expanded definition and range of preceptors. Interdisciplinary cohorts of students gained access to continua of care that included multiple medical and nursing preceptors in multiple settings engaged in outpatient practices, inpatient care, nursing homes, public health departments, school health clinics, industrial settings, and clients' homes.

This system also allowed value to be placed on contributions of nontraditional community assets such as county historians, senior and day care centers, human services agency workers, agricultural extension agents, school teachers and counselors, church leaders, and government officials. Faculty helped to develop academic community health systems and then worked within them to identify clinical and community experiences that meet educational objectives.

In one partner community, teen pregnancy and nutrition issues were raised as targets for action by student, faculty, and community member teams. In the other partner community, farm safety and school health interventions were presented as needs that could be addressed by participants. In both communities, residents participate in the planning and implementation of the "Introduction to Rural Health" course. They accommodate students in their homes during the week-long activity, offer tours of the area, and provide historical and cultural lectures through storytellers.

Senior faculty members of the three DHS colleges were the initial planners of the interdisciplinary curriculum. They became an interface between the deans and the college curriculum committees, and some senior faculty became course directors for the initial implementation of the new courses.

As curricular responsibilities grew and the number of course offerings increased, a second group of faculty was specifically recruited for full-time positions in the partnership communities. Their role was to teach the interdisciplinary curriculum; engage in professional practice or community service, serving as role models for their students; and engage in community-based research.

Each college found these new faculty, who came to ETSU specifically to become part of this unique effort, were invaluable in helping integrate the program into the community. They quickly became engaged in all facets of community life, with some faculty choosing to live in the assigned communities. Some practiced in the primary care settings attached to the college of nursing or the college of medicine; others became community leaders active in civic organizations and health-related projects. For a time, they taught in church basements and around their dining room tables; later, communities provided adequate space for teaching through renovation or new construction of facilities. Each dean kept a commitment to recognize the new roles of these faculty members in the promotion and tenure process.

To supplement the community-based faculty, some campus-based professors travel to the sites weekly. In addition, community preceptors (physicians, nurses, and allied health professionals) provide thousands of volunteer hours supervising student clinical experiences in their practices and agencies. The personal and professional backgrounds of the faculty who participated in the project follow.

- 40% grew up in rural communities.
- 35% were originally from Appalachian counties.
- 60% had previous rural practice experience.
- 35% had previous interdisciplinary practice experience.
- 30% had previous rural teaching experience.
- 35% had previous interdisciplinary teaching experience.
- 64% had been involved with a rural or interdisciplinary training experience.

Organizational Structure

As part of the Community Partnerships Program, ETSU established the Office of Rural and Community Health as its partnership structure (Richards 1996). The office formally became part of the Division of Health Sciences in 1992. It was organized with a governing board of seven persons, including the three health science deans and four community representatives (two from the Advisory Board formed in each county). A sense of trust was created by university approval of a structure in which the community had a majority vote and responsibility for budget approval; hiring of the office's executive director; and direction of curricular,

Figure 2
Expanded Community Partnerships Model Program: Dual Targets for Action

Institutional Change Targets

Community Change Targets

program evaluation, operational, and policy issues.

County Advisory Boards were formed by local leaders. Health care and other community interests were represented, including governments, schools, business and industry, and churches. The boards have been tenacious in their activity. They are a ready source of volunteers and have been a bridge to acceptance of the program by community members. The boards and the university have become allies in finding support and have effectively marketed the program locally, in the state, and in the nation.

The dual membership in the partnering structure reflects the intended nature of the benefits of the program. The Com-munity Partnerships activity aims to improve community health care and health status, promote new community services, and create organizational change within the health care system. Partnerships are designed to reinforce student selection, promote collaboration among the health sciences colleges, and gain state support for this model of education. Figure 2 displays this dual benefits approach.

Influencing Health Policy for Ongoing Support

The community has been an important part of the partnership's effort to understand and promote health policy that will support a system that demands the types of health professionals being educated by the program. This has included direct involvement by community members in national, state, and regional presentations in support of the principles of the program. A seemingly endless stream of visitors has heard from community members about the importance of the partnerships. Local media have highlighted the accomplishments of the program. Elected officials and government policy makers hear repeatedly from the community about the programs. Communities have used their connections to advocate for the principles of community-based education and sustainable county health systems, including university participation. The university likewise has used lessons learned from its partnership with communities to highlight rural health, primary care reimbursement, and workforce distribution issues and solutions.

Outcomes

The worth of any activity can be measured by its outcomes. Program evaluation has been an integral part of the change process at ETSU. Accomplishments can be documented in several areas; they include institutionalization and expansion of the curriculum; continuation and expansion of community-university partnerships; improved health in communities; and student achievements.

Institutionalization and Expansion of Interdisciplinary Curriculum

The interdisciplinary curriculum has been evaluated and refined (Franks 1998). The Interdisciplinary Curriculum Committee includes a wide variety of faculty from each college. Though grant funding is long gone, the nine interdisciplinary courses are routinely scheduled, with students recruited for participation from each college. A task force, appointed by the current vice president for health affairs, is exploring methods by which two particular foci (population-based health care and professional leadership skills) can be further developed in the curriculum. The task force has also recommended opening the courses to health professions students enrolled in the traditional courses, and redesigning the interdisciplinary communications course to make it available to all division students.

Each college within the division has made fundamental changes in its traditional programs that bring them into alignment with the principles and practices of the Community Partnerships model. The entire curriculum for the bachelor of science in nursing has been restructured to give all students a community-based educational opportunity. The medical curriculum has allocated 335 hours to primary care experiences within the first two years, and has moved to small-group learning techniques. A new community health concentration within the master of public health program now includes a three-semester sequence with the same population and health problem.

A natural expansion of the interdisciplinary curriculum was to include medical residents and graduate students in nursing and public and allied health in the plan. In 1996, the Kellogg Foundation selected the division to participate in a second national grant replicating the principles of the Community Partnerships project with medical residents, nurse practitioner students, and other graduate health professions students. The experiences in the undergraduate project were instrumental in grant preparation and implementation of the new Graduate Health Professions Education (GHPE) program (Edwards and Smith 1998).

A primary GHPE goal is to develop better health-care provider teams who will become leaders in addressing quality, cost, and access issues in collaborative practices responsive to community needs. GHPE has sponsored numerous case-based graduate seminars that introduce interdisciplinary team development and address practical issues that cut across disciplinary lines. These seminars have focused on issues such as infant mortality, diversity, and cancer and tobacco use. All family medicine residents, family nurse practitioner students, and selected public and allied health graduate students participate. Other program activities include exposure to community-based best experiences in thematic areas such as school health, migrant health, geriatrics, and occupational health, and opportunities for multidisciplinary care within a network of practices throughout the three-state Appalachian region.

Long-Term Community-University Partnerships

Long-term commitments between communities and the university have continued and expanded. Under the leadership of the president of the university (formerly dean of medicine and vice president for health affairs), the concept of community-based learning has been absorbed by the general university. An additional initiative assisted by a Kellogg grant in 1998 is supporting a review of the university's general education requirements that will sponsor the development of expanded partnerships with the business, education, arts and sciences, and applied science and technology colleges with four rural communities. These partnerships will build upon the original health partnerships in Johnson and Hawkins Counties.

The primary care practices begun before and during the Community Partnerships initiative are still thriving, and have led to deeper and stronger relationships between the DHS and the two rural communities. The level of understanding, trust, and confidence that has grown through the journey toward interdisciplinarity has produced an openness to collaborations and joint venture.

One example is the Johnson County Health Center, created in 1998, which brought together the Johnson County Hospital, a tertiary care medical center, and the university primary care practices of nursing and medicine in an innovative venture that provides cost-effective and efficient health care to the community. Another partnership is an agreement with the Quillen Veterans Affairs Medical Center to provide primary care to veterans in the two partner counties. Still a third partnership that developed was a division contract with TennCare*, the largest

---

* TennCare was created in 1994 through a Section 1115 Medicaid Waiver from the Federal Health Care Financing Administration. It includes 1.287 million Medicaid beneficiaries and other persons deemed eligible because of uninsured status. The program uses a gatekeeper model and pays $3.777

managed care organization, to conduct health risk assessments of TennCare clients and use the data to improve health care in the region.

Another serendipitous aspect of partnering with communities has been the increased interest in attending ETSU, and especially enrollment in health science programs, that has resulted from the presence of students and faculty in the rural areas. One county had a 74 percent increase in high school graduate enrollment in ETSU; the second had a 48 percent increase. Young people in the counties can imagine themselves succeeding in the health professions largely because of the role models that the nursing, medical, and public and allied health students provide.

Improved health in communities. The university practices provide over 17,500 patient care visits to residents of the rural partner counties. These practices have significantly increased access to primary care, especially for TennCare enrollees. Several graduates of the Community Partnerships Program are now employed in the partner communities and are engaged as preceptors in the academic community health systems. They make a significant contribution to educating students and delivering care in an interdisciplinary framework.

In addition to primary care practice, the faculty, students, and community members have engaged in hundreds of community projects aimed at increasing awareness of health maintenance and promotion. Clinically, they have provided thousands of health screenings for community members. Although cause and effect cannot be proven, a study by Florence and Goodrow (1996) found that the use of preventive services, including prenatal care, had improved and that deaths from all causes (and specifically deaths from cardiovascular disease) had been reduced.

The presence of the university has enabled community coalitions to form. In Johnson County, a Wellness Center has emerged that adopted a holistic view to health encouraged by faculty and students. The center is focused on traditional exercise activities for all ages, promotes youth groups, and entered the realm of adult education by offering computer literacy courses. In Hawkins County, work with the Chamber of Commerce has promoted a leadership development group with a year-long curriculum developed by faculty. The current project is a campaign to organize countywide bike paths and interorganizational support for bike safety and physical fitness events.

Student achievements. The program continues to attract students interested in rural health and primary care. Students across disciplines are increasingly recruited to ETSU because of their interest in the rural health opportunities.

---

billion to nine managed care organizations and behavioral health organizations through capitated payments.

Several students who continued on in residency or graduate study at ETSU have become leaders in the GHPE initiative.

Graduates of the Community Partnership Program have had success similar to those of traditional students on licensing and professional examinations; these include medicine's United States Medical Licensing Exam (USMLE) Step 1 and Step 2 exams and nursing's national licensure examination. Faculty and preceptors have noted positive differences in the students' physical examination and communication skills, and ability to think critically in clinical situations as compared to their traditional counterparts.

Of all medical graduates who participated in the program, 96 percent have chosen primary care residency training, compared to 55 percent for traditional ETSU medical graduates (Harris et al. 1998). This percentage of graduates choosing primary care far surpasses the national average and ranked ETSU second in the country by 1998. Likewise, 58 percent of the BSN graduates have elected to practice in rural underserved areas or in community-based settings. In contrast, less than 20 percent of traditional graduates choose community practice.

Students understand roles and contributions of team members from other disciplines and value working with community members to address health problems. When students summarize the perceived value of their interdisciplinary, community-based education, they say it enables them to do the following:

- Gain exposure to a sense of continuity of care and contact with a community.
- Develop problem solving and critical thinking skills.
- Gain adequate clinical volume and primary care focus.
- Enjoy enhanced quality of teaching in rural preceptor sites and hospitals.
- Collaborate with other disciplines.
- Understand roles and strengths of other disciplines in care.
- Learn practical aspects of patient and practice management.
- Mix different types and locations of experiences (office practice, nursing home, home health, mental health center, hospitals).

Health Policy Changes

Understanding of and involvement in health policy-related issues evolved from exposure to issues raised through participation in Kellogg Foundation activities, membership in national associations and disciplinary academies. With assistance from state and national legislators, ETSU became involved in promoting issues that embodied and supported the principles of community-based, interdisciplinary education and service. Early in the partnering process, one community helped sustain a direct state appropriation to ETSU to support a community-oriented primary care model of services and education. In 1995, ETSU deans were involved in a Governor's commission to re-establish state support for graduate medical education through TennCare, which now channels funds directly to medical schools linked to accountable outcomes that promote primary care. The nursing school played a role in new 1996 legislation for nurse practitioner reimbursement that resulted in a dramatic increase in demand for NPs in regional practices. The rural communities see the university as partners in policy; together they seek ways to retain access to quality services in the uncertain environment of financial change that has plagued other unorganized health delivery systems in rural communities throughout the nation.

LESSONS LEARNED

Separate from the direct outcomes of the project are the lessons ETSU participants have learned (and are still learning!) that may benefit others. Committed visionary leadership is necessary, requiring thinking beyond one's own discipline and college and working visibly for the whole of interdisciplinary outcomes. Attention to communication and the process of the journey is important to assure involvement, investment, and integration of ideas and relationships. Be prepared to be surprised, and challenged, both by friends who want to move farther and faster and the naysayers who don't believe at all in the principles of interdisciplinary, community-based learning. This leadership includes community partners who will learn about academic policies and politics over time, and will help educators, students, and community partners alike keep a focus on the challenge of growing new relationships and connections.

Adoption of community-based education requires a slow but steady normative change that promotes institutionalization of the value of innovation, teamwork, and accountability. Adopting interdisciplinary teaching and practice also requires change at the professional, personal, and institutional practice levels. Not all parts of the academic health center or its community partners will be ready when you are. The decade-long journey of ETSU's Division of Health Sciences underscores how important to success is congruence of institutional mission, external support, internal flexibility, and a sense of purpose enmeshed with community needs and assets. Deans, faculty, students, and community must also be ready to work collaboratively to allow failure, to improve, and to ultimately succeed in changing health professions education programs.

WORK CITED

Behringer, B., G. Burkett, W. Butler, and D. Taylor. 1996. What goes in has a great deal to do with what comes out. *Community* May:2–7.

Bishop, W.S. 1998. Organizational Dynamics as a Catalyst to Institutional Change or Why the Community Partnership Initiative was Successful in East Tennessee. Presentation to Primary Care Education for the 21st Century: Lessons from National Initiative. Baltimore, September 26.

Bondurant, S. 1995. Health care reform continues: Theses for academic medicine. *Academic Medicine* (70)2:93–97.

COGME (Council on Graduate Medical Education). 1992. *Third Report: Improving Access to Health Care Through Physician Workforce Reform.* Washington: Government Printing Office.

Edwards, J. and P. Smith. 1998. Impact of interdisciplinary education in underserved areas: Health professions collaboration in rural Tennessee. *Journal of Professions Nursing* (14)3:144–49.

Edwards, J., P. Stanton, and W. Bishop. 1998. Interdisciplinarity: The story of a journey. *Nursing and Health Care Perspectives* (19)2:116–17.

Florence, J. and B. Goodrow. 1996. *Morbidity and Mortality in Two East Tennessee Counties, 1991–1996.* A report provided to East Tennessee State University Kellogg Program. Johnson City, TN: East Tennessee State University.

Franks, R. 1998. Sustainability of Workforce Programs Beyond Foundation Support. Presentation to Primary Care Education for the 21st Century: Lessons from National Initiative. Baltimore, September 26.

Goodrow, B., C. Pullen, and R. Duggins. 1996. The road rally: An application of inquiry based learning. *Health Education* (27)2:17–25.

Harris, D., S. Starnaman, R. Henry, and C. Bland. 1998. Alternative approaches to program evaluation. *Academic Medicine* (73)10:s13–15.

Ibrahin, M., R. House, and R. Levine. 1995. Educating the public health work force for the 21st Century. *Family and Community Health* (18)3:17–25.

Olive, K., B. Goodrow, and S. Virgin. 1998. A model rural health orientation course using interdisciplinary, community oriented, inquiry based strategies. *Advances in Health Sciences Education* 3:141–52.

Shugars, D.A., E.H. O'Neil, and J.D. Baders. 1991. *Healthy America: Practitioners for 2005.* Durham, NC: The Pew Health Professions Commission.

Physician Payment Review Commission. 1994. *Annual Report to Congress, 1994.* Washington: Government Printing Office.

Richards, R., ed. 1996. *Building Partnerships: Educating Health Professionals for the Communities They Serve.* San Francisco: Jossey-Bass.

Stanton, P.E. 1998. Using Social and Organizational Change for Educational Reform: How Can an Institution Fuel and Sustain Innovation. Presentation to Primary Care Education for the 21st Century: Lessons from National Initiative. Baltimore, September 26.

Virgin, S., B. Goodrow, and R. Duggins. 1996. Scavenger hunt: An inquiry based learning exercise. *Nursing Educator* (21)5:32–34.

———. 1997. An interdisciplinary approach to community based learning: Community crossword puzzle. *Nursing and Health Care Perspectives,* December: 302-07.

5

Building an Interdisciplinary Culture

Raymond S. Greenberg, MD, PhD, and
Janis P. Bellack, PhD, RN, FAAN

The Medical University of South Carolina (MUSC), the state's only institution of higher education focused exclusively on the health professions, is the center of the state's largest health sciences complex. Located in Charleston, MUSC is home to the oldest medical school in the southern United States. Since its founding in 1824, the university has grown from a small medical facility to a comprehensive health sciences institution with a 600-bed referral and teaching center and six academic colleges: Dental Medicine, Graduate Studies, Health Professions, Medicine, Nursing, and Pharmacy. With more than 1,100 full-time faculty, these six colleges offer a wide array of undergraduate, graduate, and postdoctoral academic programs to more than 2,300 students each year.

The university's mission is to preserve and optimize human life in South Carolina and beyond. It is committed to achieving this mission through the education of future and practicing health professionals and biomedical scientists, the conduct of research in the health sciences, the delivery of patient care (with special attention to underserved populations), and service to the state as a resource in health policy, economic development, and public education and outreach.

HISTORY OF INTERDISCIPLINARY LEARNING

Historically, the university was organized as a traditional model of six independent colleges whose administration, budgets, facilities, and curricula operated separately and autonomously, with limited oversight and management from central administration. Over the last decade, this long-standing tradition of "each tub on its own bottom" has gradually shifted toward a climate in which interdisciplinary consideration and collaboration are being encouraged as well as rewarded.

The university's attention to interdisciplinary issues began in earnest in 1990 with the formation of an interdisciplinary University Education Committee (UEC). This committee was charged with providing leadership for developing interdisciplinary courses and a common academic calendar. As a first step, the UEC developed and disseminated a university philosophy of education that emphasized interdisciplinary collaboration as a core educational value, as follows:

> The learning process should facilitate an understanding and appreciation of the unique and valuable contributions of each professional discipline. The educational experiences of all students should incorporate opportunities for interdisciplinary dialogue and collaboration in classroom, clinical, and social settings.

This commitment was brought to life in 1992 when UEC, with support from the vice president for academic affairs, convened a university-wide retreat to address opportunities and challenges for educational change across the university's six colleges. The two-day retreat involved more than two hundred faculty, administrators, and students. It was patterned on the theme of the first report of the Pew Health Professions Commission, *Healthy America: Practitioners for 2005;* a major thrust of the report was the need to reduce barriers to interprofessional collaboration: "Universities should encourage programmatic efforts that address health and health professional educational issues across traditional boundaries of the health professions" (Shugars et al. 1991).

Facilitated by an external consultant, fifteen interdisciplinary work groups met during the retreat to identify major issues the university should address to ready itself and its graduates for the twenty-first century of health care delivery. For the first time in the university's history, faculty from the six colleges were formally invited to come together around educational issues of cross-disciplinary importance and to collaborate in generating ideas for improving interdisciplinary learning opportunities in the university's academic programs. During the retreat, the need to achieve greater interdisciplinary collaboration in the educational process was identified as one of eight major challenges. The other seven were as follows: core competencies, community-based experiences, outcomes assessment, diversity, faculty development, teaching incentives and rewards, and educational technology and support services.

Although interdisciplinary experiences were singled out as a particular challenge for the educational enterprise, their cross-disciplinary relevance and implicit potential for interdisciplinary solutions characterized all eight challenges.

Subsequent to the retreat, an office of educational planning was established by the vice president for academic affairs to oversee interdisciplinary strategic planning for educational change. The investment of substantial resources by the university's academic leadership in both the retreat and the creation of a permanent office to ensure continuing efforts made a public statement about the institution's commitment to educational change and was critical to subsequent accomplishments. As Conner (1995) notes, "A committed sponsor recognizes the demand that a change project makes on organizational resources . . . and will publicly commit these resources."

The university subsequently sought and received two small training grants from the Center for the Health Professions, home of the Pew Health Professions Commission, to support start-up strategic planning efforts and provide leadership training for five interdisciplinary teams charged with implementing strategic plan initiatives. The university's interdisciplinary approach to broad-based strategic planning for educational reform was instrumental in securing this early support from the center.

Specifically, the five implementation teams were charged with steering ongoing efforts around several key issues, one of which was fostering interdisciplinary learning in community-based settings. Team members worked collaboratively to raise awareness and identify opportunities for interdisciplinary education within their respective colleges. One early, successful effort involved faculty and students from the Colleges of Medicine, Dental Medicine, Nursing, and Pharmacy coming together to plan interdisciplinary experiences in an urban underserved community near the university; they were not electives or add-ons but part of each college's core curriculum. Students from the first-year "Introduction to Clinical Medicine" course, the dental school's community outreach component, the third-year undergraduate "Community Health Nursing" course, and an undergraduate community pharmacy rotation were involved. Key people from the community, including a neighborhood association president, community agency heads, and AmeriCorps volunteers were also part of the planning, thus broadening the definition of "interdisciplinary" to include the community and to assure that the experiences would address community needs as well as student learning.

CREATING AN INTERDISCIPLINARY CULTURE

In the ensuing years, the focus and emphasis on interdisciplinary activities has grown substantially. Most of the early efforts occurred at the grass-roots level; their success was due to a core group of faculty committed to the value of interdisciplinary experiences for student learning and preparation for professional practice. These "early adopters" led the way in designing and building successful interdisciplinary learning experiences that, in turn, generated student enthusiasm and demand for more such experiences and sparked broader faculty interest.

In addition, success in building an interdisciplinary culture is attributable to key support from institutional administrators and academic leaders, including the vice president for academic affairs, the dean of the College of Medicine, and the executive director of the South Carolina Area Health Education Consortium. They articulated a vision for interdisciplinary education and created a climate conducive to innovation and experimentation by faculty and students. Most important, they dedicated resources to its accomplishment. This commitment and the accompanying resources have provided visible and vital support for several interdisciplinary initiatives over the last several years that could not have happened without dedicated resources. Two examples are illustrative.

Strategic Planning

In early 1997, a university-wide planning committee was appointed and charged with developing a comprehensive, integrated strategic plan to guide the university's efforts and allocation of resources over the next three to five years (www.musc.edu/plan/index.html). Five organizing themes were identified in advance by university leadership. "Emphasize interdisciplinary approaches" was one of them. This public proclamation of the value of interdisciplinary efforts directed the planning group to focus on increasing interdisciplinary and intercollegiate course work and experiences. As a result, after several iterations and input from the full university community, the final strategic plan included several action strategies aimed at advancing interdisciplinary education, as follows:

1. Institute a service-learning requirement that is both community based and interdisciplinary in all degree-granting programs.

2. Create incentives and rewards for faculty and student participation in interdisciplinary and community-based educational experiences.

3. Ensure that all curricula are designed to prepare students and residents with a set of core competencies, including the ability to "work effectively in interdisciplinary teams."

4. Charge each college to develop and offer at least one university-wide

interdisciplinary course that fosters acquisition of one or more of the core competencies.

Efforts are underway in all colleges and academic programs to address these challenges.

The Healthy South Carolina Initiative

Also in 1997, an internal grants program— the Healthy South Carolina Initiative (www.musc.edu/hsci)—was launched by the vice president for academic affairs, with funding from the President's Council, to encourage the faculty's community outreach efforts. One of the criteria for evaluating proposals for funding was evidence of interdisciplinary collaboration involving faculty and students from two or more colleges. Twenty-eight projects were funded through a competitive peer-review process and are underway.

These kinds of projects address health concerns of vulnerable populations, and many involve faculty and students in learning the value of an interdisciplinary team approach to health care in partnership with the community. In fact, more than a third (n = ten) of the twenty-eight projects explicitly involve faculty and students from more than one college, and two others are being implemented in collaboration with two local public institutions: the College of Charleston and The Citadel.

One project, the Enterprise/MUSC Neighborhood Health Program, involves all five clinical colleges plus the MUSC library. This program includes a partnership for hypertension and diabetes management and education whereby faculty and students from the Colleges of Nursing, Dental Medicine, Health Professions, Medicine, and Pharmacy work collaboratively with community partners in eighteen inner-city neighborhoods. The program is designed to improve the way people find out they have diabetes and hypertension

MUSC Core Competencies

Curricula at the Medical University of South Carolina must be designed to ensure that students, residents, and fellows are prepared with the following set of core competencies:

- Communicate effectively.
- Provide humanistic care that involves persons and their families in decisions about their health care.
- Value diversity and demonstrate sensitivity to diversity issues in all professional behaviors.
- Use information technology and manage large volumes of knowledge.
- Apply critical thinking skills to solve problems.
- Make ethical decisions in health care, education, and research.
- Work effectively in interdisciplinary teams.
- Understand population-based care and clinical epidemiology.
- Promote health optimization and prevention of disease.
- Practice effectively in the evolving health care system with an understanding of its economics and management.
- Use clinical practice guidelines.
- Continuously improve health and health care.
- Value and engage in lifelong learning.

—MUSC Strategic Plan, 1997

and assist them in reducing risk factors, managing their diseases and preventing complications, and learning how to live longer and healthier lives with these diseases.

Recently, the executive director of the national Community-Campus Partnerships for Health visited the MUSC campus and Neighborhood Health Program sites. Her comment: "I have not come across another academic health center that is attempting this level of community involvement across the disciplines and a wide variety of community partners" (Dr. Sarena Seifer, personal communication, March 16, 1999). Some other examples of funded interdisciplinary projects follow:

The university places high value on ensuring that its graduates embrace a commitment to serve the public and to work effectively with other health professionals.

Cervical Cancer Education and Prevention Project—Students from the Colleges of Nursing and Medicine participate in learning about women's health in interdisciplinary experiences in local health departments. This project focuses on providing services to high-risk, low-income African American women.

Innovative Alternatives for Women—Students and faculty from the Colleges of Nursing, Dental Medicine, Health Professions, Medicine, and Pharmacy provide integrated health care services, including child care, dental care, and primary health care to women receiving public assistance. The women are enrolled in a twelve-week occupational skills training program.

Adaptive Aquatics—Students from the College of Health Professions physical therapy and occupational therapy programs and the College of Charleston physical education program work together to teach swimming to children with disabilities and special needs. The program aims to reduce the incidence of drowning accidents in this population while improving their mobility, social skills, mental skills, and quality of life.

An Interdisciplinary School-Based Training Site for Health Professional Students—Faculty from the Colleges of Nursing and Medicine provide comprehensive primary care to inner-city high school students in a school-based clinic, and health education for school classes and the community. The clinic also provides interdisciplinary community-based learning experiences for students in the Colleges of Medicine, Nursing, Pharmacy, Dental Medicine, and Health Professions.

Integrated Health Care Services for Women and Children—Faculty from the Colleges of Nursing and Medicine provide primary health care, including prenatal care, services to women and children in a rural, underserved community outside of Charleston. The program also provides the students from the Colleges of

Medicine and Nursing with the opportunity to learn an integrated, interdisciplinary model of care to improve the health status of this rural population.

Other Projects and Programs

Other small examples of visible leadership for interdisciplinary education and community service abound.

A student-initiated community volunteer program, MUSC Gives Back, was created in 1993 to provide opportunities for students from all six colleges to work in interdisciplinary teams on a variety of community projects. Funded initially by the College of Medicine and a grant from the Corporation for National Service, MUSC Gives Back now has a permanent office in the university's Harper Student Center and is funded and administered centrally. Since its inception, more than 2,000 student volunteers from every college on campus have collectively donated nearly 30,000 hours of community service to more than two hundred community agencies.

Collaborating students from the Colleges of Health Professions, Graduate Studies, and Medicine have assisted with construction of Habitat for Humanity homes on one of the rural sea islands south of Charleston.

Students from a variety of colleges have collaborated to provide health education and screening at periodic community health and immunization fairs offered by the university or other community organizations.

Students from the Colleges of Medicine and Nursing completed interdisciplinary training to serve as labor coaches for the Florence Crittendon Program for Unwed Mothers and counsel victims of rape through People Against Rape, a local community coalition.

Students from the Colleges of Health Professions, Medicine, and Pharmacy worked in interdisciplinary teams as tutors for students at a local middle school. Half of the middle school students improved their math scores following a semester of tutoring. A secondary goal was to interest inner-city middle school students in health professions careers.

The university places high value on ensuring that its graduates embrace a commitment to serve the public and to work effectively with other health professionals. Students who are preparing for careers as practicing health professionals are expected to abide by the following "Health Professions Covenant" of the Association of Academic Health Centers, of which the university is a member. It reads as follows:

> As a health care professional dedicated to enhancing the well-being of individuals and communities, I am committed to achieving and sustaining the highest level of professional competence, to fulfilling my responsibilities with compas-

sion for patients' suffering, and to helping patients make their own informed choices about health care whenever possible. Recognizing that effective health promotion, disease prevention, and curative and long-term care are products of the combined efforts of teams of health professionals, I pledge collaboration with all of my colleagues similarly committed to meeting the health care needs of individuals and their communities. Further, I will work within my profession to encourage placement of the patient's and the public's interests above the self-interests of my individual profession.

At the request of the University Education Committee, in 1995 the university adopted the Health Professions Covenant as its code of conduct for interdisciplinary education and practice. The code was published in the university catalog, student handbooks, and the annual commencement program. Students are introduced to the Covenant during new-student orientation sessions.

With leadership from the executive director of the South Carolina AHEC and the dean of the College of Medicine, funds were made available beginning in 1994 to support the participation of the university and the South Carolina AHEC in a national interdisciplinary professional education collaborative sponsored by the Institute for Healthcare Improvement (IHI). The aim of the national collaborative is to improve health, health care and health professions education—especially interdisciplinary education—through the use of continuous improvement methods. An interdisciplinary faculty team (from family medicine, nursing, health administration, and pharmacy) was formed to work locally to achieve the aims of the collaborative.

Over the past five years, the team has piloted several interdisciplinary learning experiences that were subsequently integrated into selected MUSC academic programs. For example, the team worked with faculty and community preceptors to integrate interdisciplinary continuous improvement into a rural interdisciplinary practicum offered each summer in collaboration with the Low Country AHEC. The team also developed and offered an elective course, "Continuous Improvement in Health Care: An Interdisciplinary Learning Experience." The team is currently focusing its efforts on implementing a required, interdisciplinary primary care rural clerkship for third-year medical students.

In early 1998, the dean of the College of Medicine implemented five criteria for clinical site development for a newly instituted Deans' Primary Care Rural Clerkship. One criterion is that the site must provide an opportunity for interdisciplinary education and practice. This clerkship was required of all third-year medical students beginning July 1999 and operated in collaboration with the University of South Carolina medical school in Columbia. Although the mix of providers varies by site, students are working with advanced nurse practitioners,

Table 1
Sample Humanitas Entries, (Vols. II & III)

Prose/Essay	Contributor
Did We Do the Right Thing?	College of Medicine faculty
Donor	Medical Center staff
Retirement Day	College of Medicine faculty
Coming to Carolina	College of Nursing faculty
Sunset of My Childhood Home	College of Pharmacy student
Emerging Infectious Diseases: Philosophy & Theology	College of Medicine student
Poetry	
Morning	College of Nursing faculty
Learning to Walk	College of Health Professions student
Passions	Medical Center staff
The Einstein Nutcracker	College of Graduate Studies faculty
Photography	
Where Aunt Helen Lives	Provost's Office staff
English Monastery	College of Health Professions student
His World	Medical Center staff
Shadow Dancing	College of Graduate Studies student

certified nurse midwives, physician assistants, pharmacists, nutritionists, diabetes educators, and health administrators in addition to their primary care physician preceptors. At some sites, students are also working with health professions students in these disciplines, including those from MUSC as well as other professional schools in the state. The next step of the primary care rural clerkship will focus on incorporating students from other MUSC programs, particularly the nurse practitioner, nurse midwifery, physician assistant, and doctor of pharmacy programs.

In 1998, an interdisciplinary university-level Clinical Sites Coordinating Committee was created by the vice president for academic affairs to facilitate community-based site development and student placement. Specific attention was given to ensuring opportunities for interdisciplinary education and practice. Evaluation of both on- and off-campus clinical sites is under way to determine their capacity for supporting interdisciplinary education and interest in doing so.

For the past two years, the vice president for academic affairs has allocated university funds to supplement a Federally funded rural interdisciplinary practicum offered by the Low Country AHEC in collaboration with the Colleges of Health Professions, Medicine, Nursing, and Pharmacy. The aim is to double the number of students who could participate in the project.

Since 1997, university funds have been allocated by the vice president for academic affairs to support the publication each spring of an interdisciplinary humanities journal, *Humanitas*. The publication's purpose is to encourage expression "of the values, interests and cherished preoccupations of the MUSC community." Submissions by students, faculty, and staff are reviewed and selected by students in the Medical Humanities Scholars Program and faculty from the interdisciplinary University Humanities Committee (table 1). The third issue of *Humanitas* is available on the MUSC Web site (www.edtest.musc.edu/humanitas/humanitas.htm).

The steering group for a university facilities master planning process, begun in 1998, has charged planners to design future physical facilities with a view to improving opportunities and areas that foster interdisciplinary interaction in education, research, and student life.

A Center for Healthcare Research was established in 1996 with dedicated start-up funds to foster and support health services research, and to train investigators in interdisciplinary approaches to health services research. It was originally planned as a department within the College of Medicine, but the vice president for academic affairs determined that it should be housed centrally in an interdisciplinary manner, and allocated funds for its creation and initial support. One of the center's aims is "to develop a cadre of investigators of sufficient number, education, interdisciplinary mix, and experience to move the center's agenda forward." The center's administrative and research teams involve faculty from all six colleges.

An existing Center for the Study of Aging was reorganized in 1999 by the vice president for academic affairs to promote greater interdisciplinary collaboration in education, research, and practice.

CHALLENGES TO CHANGE

Despite these many successes, our journey in creating an interdisciplinary culture has not been without struggle and conflict. Many faculty are involved in and committed to interdisciplinary activities in their teaching, research, and clinical practice. But barriers to full participation persist. Most are present at other academic health centers as well.

A significant barrier has been the way tuition revenues are generated and returned to the colleges. Courses at any of the six colleges generate revenues at much higher rates than do those labeled "interdisciplinary." Furthermore, there is no mechanism for allocating funds back to the home department or college of faculty members who participate in teaching a course offered by another college or department. To date, interdisciplinary teaching has been largely voluntary, over and above the faculty member's regular teaching assignment. Thus, faculty members do not receive credit in their home department for interdisciplinary teaching outside their department unless the chair chooses to reward such participation.

Interdisciplinary teaching also places greater demands on faculty time because it involves more collaboration and coordination with the other members of the teaching team; this additional preparation time is not typically explicitly considered in workload calculations.

We are currently working on an alternative mechanism for funding interdisciplinary courses to provide incentives for departments who offer such courses and for faculty who participate in them. Meanwhile, a large cadre of faculty have been doing so without special incentives, attesting to the interdisciplinary spirit growing on campus.

Scheduling conflict has perhaps been the greatest barrier to creating interdisciplinary learning experiences. Although the university follows a core academic calendar, academic programs operate on different course schedules within established academic terms. For example, some programs operate on a schedule of four-week clinical rotations, whereas others adhere to a semester-length schedule of rotations, making it impossible to create interdisciplinary student-learning teams that have consistent membership over time. Although we have imagined a day when we might adopt similar clinical rotation schedules across the colleges, such a change is not likely to occur in the foreseeable future.

We realize, and for now have accepted, the many curricular and disciplinary barriers to creating a true common calendar. Therefore, we have begun to look for opportunities to structure interdisciplinary learning experiences at times and in places where students are together in the same clinical setting. For example, at a rural clinical practice, medical students and physician assistant students rotate every four weeks while a nurse practitioner student is in the setting for fifteen weeks. Since there are students from at least two and sometimes three disciplines in the practice at the same time, faculty and community-based preceptors will be working on creating a more explicit focus on interdisciplinary interaction around patients and problems that students encounter in common. As students rotate in and out of the practice, those already in the setting will be able to serve as a resource to those who are new; the once-new students, in turn, will be a resource to those in a subsequent rotation. In this way, all will have planned interdisciplinary experiences focused on learning to work effectively in interdisciplinary teams, assuring they acquire this important core competency now expected of all MUSC graduates.

DEANS ADVOCATE FOR CHANGE

The greatest impetus for advancing interdisciplinary education is likely to come from the campus deans, who recently developed and endorsed a plan to achieve the interdisciplinary goals and strategies outlined in the university's strategic plan. The Deans' Council predicated its recommendations on the following assumptions:

■ Interdisciplinary education is different and more complex than multidisciplinary education. It requires communication among disciplines, an appreciation and understanding of other professional perspectives, and an integration of multiple perspectives toward a common goal or problem. This approach requires careful curriculum design and considerable faculty commitment and time, and thus, should be undertaken with attention to its effectiveness.

■ Interdisciplinary learning should occur in multiple venues, including formal and informal curricula, research, clinical practice, and student life. The culture of the institution must support interdisciplinary learning and appreciation of diverse perspectives.

■ Consideration should be given to determining the most valuable and necessary applications of interdisciplinary learning, i.e., which competencies require an interdisciplinary perspective, which disciplines should be brought together around which issues, and which methods are best suited to foster interdisciplinary learning. A curriculum design process to address these issues will take time and must be continually evaluated for effectiveness.

■ Despite the commitment to interdisciplinary learning, not all efforts need to or should involve all disciplines.

■ Known barriers to interdisciplinary learning include scheduling; curriculum change processes; credit-hour differences; discipline-specific requirements; lack of faculty interdisciplinary expertise, financing, and incentives; and professional myopia, all of which must be addressed if true interdisciplinary learning is to be achieved.

Given these assumptions, the Deans' Council adopted the following recommendations aimed at expanding and strengthening interdisciplinary activities at MUSC.

■ Identify and implement interdisciplinary courses, with each college choosing a focus and discipline mix deemed most essential and natural for interdisciplinary education for its one or more disciplines.

■ Develop a virtual course/learning experience in selected content areas (e.g., health care ethics, continuous improvement in health care, health promotion and disease prevention, population health) produced by an interdisciplinary team of faculty in collaboration with the multimedia production staff and resources in the university's educational technology lab.

■ Evaluate existing and future clinical learning sites for their capacity to provide interdisciplinary clinical education involving all relevant disciplines.

■ Foster intermingling of professional disciplines in such areas as university social events and facilities master planning.

■ Create an infrastructure that supports and rewards interdisciplinary research.

These recommendations coming from the campus's academic leadership group are believed to be key to future success. Without commitment from those in positions to allocate resources, it is unlikely that interdisciplinary learning will become an integral part of the institutional culture. Many faculty have been working at a grass-roots level to create and implement interdisciplinary learning experiences, often with great success. However, there must also be sustained commitment from the leadership, accompanied by appropriate incentives and rewards. Faculty committed to advancing interdisciplinary education and life at the university must not be disadvantaged when it comes to annual evaluations or promotion and tenure decisions. Leadership and specific support from the academic deans will help ensure that faculty are appropriately acknowledged and rewarded for their interdisciplinary efforts.

LESSONS LEARNED

Over the past six years, MUSC has made significant progress in creating a culture that champions and supports interdisciplinary education and practice. Many efforts have been successful, but we have also learned what does not work. We share ten lessons below in the hope that they may provide valuable insights for other academic health centers and health professions education programs as they work to expand and improve interdisciplinary efforts on their own campuses.

1. *Develop a common definition of "interdisciplinary," communicate it throughout the institution, and use it consistently.* Interdisciplinary can mean different things to different people and is often used interchangeably with "multidisciplinary." Interdisciplinary is also sometimes used to refer to different subspecialties of the same discipline working together, for example, physicians in internal

medicine collaborating with physicians in surgery or orthopedics. However, interdisciplinary is more than and qualitatively differs from multidisciplinary or intradisciplinary (subsets of the same discipline) approaches to education and practice (table 2).

It became apparent during early interdisciplinary planning efforts at MUSC that we needed to define what we meant by this term and communicate it to all involved to ensure common use and understanding. In 1993, an Interdisciplinary Learning Task Force defined interdisciplinary as "a group of participants from various disciplines working together to solve a common problem, involving real interactions, reciprocal exchanges, the integration of concepts and methods, and, as a result, mutual enhancement. Its hallmark is a problem-solving experience in which each professional grows beyond disciplinary and professional boundaries to arrive at a common solution." This definition was shared with key constituents within the university and used by the planning groups in their educational change efforts.

2. *Where possible, integrate interdisciplinary experiences into the required curriculum rather than add them as electives.* Although interdisciplinary electives are likely to enrich any student's curriculum, the intense program of study and the inflexible, lock-step nature of most health professions curricula limit the opportunity for students to take advantage of such electives. Offering interdisciplinary experiences as separate and stand-alone entities, or limiting them to a few special experiences divorced from the mainstream of required educational experiences,

Table 2
Differences Between 'Multidisciplinary' and 'Interdisciplinary'

Multidisciplinary	Interdisciplinary
Professional roles and responsibilities clearly and separately delineated	Professional roles and responsibilities shared
Ownership of unique knowledge and skills	Shared core of knowledge and skills
Hierarchical authority	Shared authority (all team members; anyone can be the leader, depending on situational needs)
Independent	Interdependent
Responsibility for own discipline's practice and outcomes	Responsibility for shared practice and outcomes of team
Limited to care providers	Broad-based; includes patient, family, and community agencies as well as a range of care providers

conveys the message that interdisciplinary work is unique and different from usual practice. Instead, interdisciplinary learning opportunities and experiences should be woven into the curriculum. Faculty should look for, create, and take advantage of all possible ways to achieve this situation, including structured clinical experiences, student life programs and activities, interdisciplinary seminar series, and bringing students together from different disciplines to learn and gain experience in core competencies.

For example, a small interdisciplinary group of students can be assigned to learn about community-driven and population-based approaches to health care around a specific community health need—Building interdisciplinary learning experiences into the required curriculum, defining expectations, and holding students accountable for effective interdisciplinary teamwork, conveys the value the institution places on this important competency.

3. *Review curricula and clinical sites for experiences that best lend themselves to interdisciplinary learning. Interdisciplinary experiences are more likely to be successful in community-based settings where practice sites are not bound by the departmental divisions and hierarchies of the academic health center.* We have found that community-based practice sites are also more open to using interdisciplinary approaches to delivering health care, especially when these approaches can be shown to be beneficial to the practice site and the people and community served.

Nontraditional settings especially can benefit from interdisciplinary models of care (e.g., delivery of care to special populations with unmet health needs). For example, faculty and staff from the Colleges of Nursing and Medicine jointly created and manage a school-based clinic at an inner-city high school close to the MUSC campus. The school serves primarily low-income students whose families are uninsured or underinsured. Interdisciplinary teams of students from nursing, medicine, health professions, pharmacy, and dental medicine have selected experiences as part of their required curricula, working with this high school population to provide comprehensive primary care services as well as individual and community health education.

4. *Introduce students to interdisciplinary experiences early.* Ideally, students should be engaged in interdisciplinary experiences from the start of their program of study—that is, before they become isolated in their discipline-specific domains and "tainted" by traditional disciplinary hierarchies, boundaries, and biases. At MUSC, we have begun to incorporate interdisciplinary opportunities for interaction in new-student orientation activities, with a specific emphasis on taking advantage of the MUSC Gives Back program so that students can volunteer in interdisciplinary teams for community service. Engaging students in required interdisciplinary learning experiences in the first year of the required curriculum

may be even more valuable; in the example described earlier, students enrolled in "Introduction to Clinical Medicine" have interdisciplinary experiences in an urban underserved community with students from several other disciplines.

5. *Capitalize on student interest and enthusiasm for working together and learning from each other.* Students come to health professions educational experiences with few predetermined biases about how health professionals learn and practice together. Our experience has been that the students are much more open to the incorporation of interdisciplinary experiences in the curriculum than are the faculty; the latter must unlearn what they know as well as learn what they don't know. In fact, students are often the leaders and drivers of such change. The MUSC Gives Back program is an excellent example of a student-initiated program that was designed at the outset, by students, to create opportunities to work across colleges and disciplinary boundaries to serve community needs.

6. *Support and recognize early adopters who have instituted successful interdisciplinary experiences.* In any type of change, there will be individuals who lead the pack. These early adopters can be instrumental in spreading innovation throughout an organization when they are successful and if others become aware of their work. In addition to making personal acknowledgments of this work, featuring successful interdisciplinary ventures of early adopters in the campus newspaper or on the institution's Web site can be a valuable way to recognize these people and spread awareness of their work throughout the organization. A full-color brochure of the twenty-eight projects of the Healthy South Carolina Initiative, featuring a number of the early faculty leaders in interdisciplinary education, was produced and disseminated recently to a broad audience within MUSC as well as to key community partners and leaders.

Another mechanism for supporting early adopters is to offer faculty development opportunities that bring faculty from different disciplines together around a common academic issue. At MUSC, twenty early adopter faculty (three from each college and two from Library Sciences and Informatics) received support to attend an interactive workshop on developing Web-based courses. Many have continued to assist each other in incorporating educational technologies into their teaching. Interdisciplinary campus round tables on teaching technologies and community-based interdisciplinary education have been another mechanism for creating and sustaining an interdisciplinary faculty culture.

7. *Create incentives and rewards that encourage faculty participation in interdisciplinary activities.* One of the most frequently cited barriers to interdisciplinary ventures in academic health centers is the lack of incentives and rewards for interdisciplinary teaching, research, practice, and service. In fact, promotion, tenure, and annual evaluation criteria, mechanisms for allocating credit for teach-

ing workload and indirect costs from funded research, and the invisibility of much of the time and effort that go into creating successful interdisciplinary activities serve as countervailing forces in most institutions.

Faculty and administrators must work together to change faculty evaluation, promotion, and tenure guidelines so they recognize and reward faculty involvement in interdisciplinary teaching, community service, research, and publication; for example, they could assign equal value to the contributions of all investigators and authors for their interdisciplinary work instead of counting only senior authorship or principal investigator status. Designating institutional funds for special educational, research, or community outreach initiatives or projects, with a stipulation that they be interdisciplinary and to which faculty or departments can apply, can be a powerful incentive, as MUSC discovered with its Healthy South Carolina Initiative.

Another recent example has been initiation of a university-wide orientation program for new faculty, which brings new faculty from all colleges together to meet each other, share information about themselves, network, and learn about the institution's organization, culture, and resources. Feedback from attendees has been quite positive, and nearly all have commented on the value of meeting faculty who are not in their own departments and colleges. Several have followed up on these initial contacts and are working together on teaching or research issues of common interest.

8. *Recognize that sponsorship from key academic leaders is critical to successful institutionalization of interdisciplinary learning, and keep them informed.* The actual planning for and implementation of interdisciplinary experiences typically occurs at a grass-roots level. Therefore, it is important that faculty and others responsible for advancing interdisciplinary education cultivate the institution's leaders by keeping them informed about interdisciplinary efforts and successes. For example, the MUSC local interdisciplinary team affiliated with the IHI collaborative project provides a periodic written update to the project's local sponsors (dean of the College of Medicine and executive director of the South Carolina AHEC) with emphasis on actual outcomes produced as a result of their investment. Keeping an interdisciplinary project front and center with key leaders and sponsors can be crucial to its sustainability, especially when the outcomes provide documented evidence of improved education and practice.

9. *Look for and take advantage of opportunities to connect with others within and beyond the institution to share ideas and strategies and build understanding of interdisciplinary learning.* In addition to ongoing participation in the national IHI interdisciplinary collaborative, MUSC is an active institutional participant in the Group on Multiprofessional Education (GOMPE) of the Association of

Academic Health Centers. This group affords MUSC a continuous opportunity to connect with other AHCs through the GOMPE electronic Listserv and annual face-to-face meetings, allowing us to learn about best practices at other institutions for possible adoption or adaptation to MUSC. Further, the MUSC associate provost for educational programs serves on the Advisory Committee to the Center for Interdisciplinary, Community-Based Learning (CICL) of the AHC, which benefits the university and also allows MUSC an opportunity to share its own best practices with the Association. Another example of interinstitutional connection is the virtual meetings held via teleconference that the directors of the Deans' Rural Primary Care Clerkship engaged in last year. Also taking part were several academic health centers that had already implemented successful rural interdisciplinary experiences. Many participants have subsequently adapted several ideas gleaned from the conferences for use at MUSC.

10. *Use physical space and communication technology to create and enhance interdisciplinary interaction.* The design and layout of physical space can either encourage or prohibit interdisciplinary activities and learning. With education becoming increasingly interactive, there is great opportunity for using space to foster interaction of students and faculty from different disciplines. The current MUSC facilities planning process addresses the need to design and situate new facilities and space that encourage interdisciplinary interaction in formal settings such as classrooms, microcomputer labs, and seminar rooms, as well as in informal areas such as green space, walkways, and lounge, eating, fitness, and student life facilities.

In addition, communication technologies offer tremendous opportunity and promise to improve interdisciplinary work. The Deans' Primary Care Rural Clerkship is using WebCT to post materials and communicate with students on rural rotations, giving them access to each other and to the campus-based interdisciplinary faculty team. As students encounter problems in their practice, they share cases and pose questions on the Intranet, and an interdisciplinary dialogue ensues. For instance, one student wrote:

> I met with the dietitian at Hampton Medical Center this week, and she gave me information on some diabetic cookbooks that have multiple meal plans, with recipes for different lunches and dinners for up to one month. This is exactly what the Diabetes Support Group had in mind. These books should be helpful for those with the initiative and the money. They may not be too helpful for those diabetics who are not recipe cooks. I have discovered that older patients may not use recipes in any shape or form. They cook the same way their mothers cooked. The books may not be helpful for those with limited funds as well. How can I measure an improvement in diabetes care using this information in such a short time period?

The subsequent dialogue involved two family medicine physicians, two nurse clinicians, and a diabetes educator who focused on helping the student access additional community resources, explore alternatives for patients who wouldn't use recipes or who had limited funds, consider cultural influences on how people manage chronic illness, and identify measures of improvement.

In the coming year, we plan to explore ways to take even greater advantage of technology to create virtual interdisciplinary learning experiences for students on and off campus. This strategy would include using educational media to post virtual cases to assigned interdisciplinary teams of students.

CONCLUSION

Many forces and factors are necessary to create and sustain a culture of inter-disciplinary education and practice in academic health centers, especially as the centers face daunting fiscal and organizational challenges. However, as the fourth Pew report notes, the future of health care "will call on all health professions—physicians, nurses, pharmacists, dentists, allied professionals, and public health and social workers—to work together in more focused ways" (O'Neil and the Pew Health Professions Commission 1998). We cannot neglect this responsibility. Those who are educating the future generation of health professionals must ensure that professionals-in-training have many and varied opportunities to learn and work together in interdisciplinary education and practice arrangements so they acquire the knowledge and skills for effective teamwork. The coordinated efforts of a range of health disciplines will be needed to achieve the goals of improving access, quality and cost-effectiveness of health care, reducing the social and economic burden of illness, and assuring optimal health outcomes of the public which is served by the interdisciplinary health care team.

WORK CITED

Conner, D. 1995. *Managing at the Speed of Change*, New York: Villard Books, p. 113.

O'Neil, E.H., and the Pew Health Professions Commission. 1998. *Recreating Health Professional Practice for a New Century.* San Francisco: Pew Health Professions Commission, p. 39.

Shugars, D.A., E.H. O'Neil, J.D. Bader, eds. 1991. *Healthy America: Practitioners for 2005, an Agenda for Action for U.S. Health Professional Schools.* Durham, NC: The Pew Health Professions Commission, p. 23.

6

Sharing a Common Core: Stony Brook's Program in Interprofessional Education

Peter C. Williams, JD, PhD, Ann W. Richmond, PhD, and Norman H. Edelman, MD

Too often the health professions have approached patient care in isolation from one another; it is essential that medicine, dentistry, nursing and the other health professions develop their programs of education, research and patient care in close collaboration with one another from the outset.

—Edward G. Pellegrino, MD

There is a great need for the well-established health professions to work together in a collegial environment in order to maintain standards and professionalism as they are placed under attack by a variety of "environmental" forces. It is my view that this can best be achieved by providing the opportunity for students in the various professions to work together at an early stage of their education, in order to gain respect for each other's competencies and for each other as people.

—Norman H. Edelman, MD

These two remarks were made a quarter of a century apart, one by the first vice president (Pellegrino 1972a) and the other by the current vice president (Edelman 1998) for health sciences at the State University of New York (SUNY) at Stony Brook. They express in strikingly similar language this institution's ongoing hope for interprofessional education in the interest of better patient care. There is now a renewed effort to realize that hope through new efforts to combine some aspects of the training of the students in the five health professions schools: dentistry

(SDM), health technology and management (HTM), medicine (SOM), nursing (SON), and social welfare (SSW). To understand and evaluate our current endeavors in collaborative education, one must acquire an appreciation of the political and ideological origins of the Health Sciences Center (HSC) at Stony Brook and the rather zigzag path our efforts have taken since the center's opening in 1971.

THE STAGE IS SET

Four forces came together in the mid 1960s to prompt both the opening of a new health sciences center on Long Island and, more important here, the establishment of one in which a core of interprofessional education would become a major emphasis.

> *New institutions tend to tolerate innovation more easily. A new school can be relatively free of entrenched, vested interests; patterns aren't set.*

The first factor was the nationwide belief that there was likely to be a shortage of health care providers within a few decades. More professional schools would be needed to train them. Although this was a national perception and led to the creation of more than thirty medical schools across the country, the potential shortage was of particular concern in New York.

In 1961, Governor Rockefeller appointed a special New York State Committee on Medical Education (called the Muir Committee after its chair, Malcolm Muir). In 1963, the committee submitted a report calling for a substantial increase in the number of New York graduates in all the health professions. Long Island, predominantly Republican and one of the fastest growing areas in the state, was chosen as the best place for a new health sciences school and its affiliated tertiary care hospital. Since SUNY Stony Brook, a rapidly growing research university, already existed, the Stony Brook campus was a natural locus for new health academic programs. The result was a five-school, publicly funded, health sciences center located on the campus of a new and important research university within a short distance of New York City.

A second factor permitted innovative programs in interprofessional learning at Stony Brook. New institutions tend to tolerate innovation more easily. A new school can be relatively free of entrenched, vested interests; patterns aren't set. Of most interest at Stony Brook was the desire to include collaborative education, research, and practice for various kinds of health professionals in the curriculum. It had become clear that the changing structure of health care delivery was beginning to demand teamwork among several different sorts of providers; the best way to prepare students for their increasingly integrated roles would be, as the quotations above suggest, to train health care personnel to work together—to develop the health care team.

These first two developmental influences were not unique to Stony Brook, although their expression here has had some unique characteristics. The third factor was somewhat less ubiquitous: the belief in the value of a new kind of interdisciplinary education integrating social sciences and humanities within traditional science and clinical instruction.* Growing consideration was given in the late 60s to social issues raised by technological advances, in particular to those issues arising out of research involving human subjects. Allocation and overuse of remarkable technical resources began to attract public as well as professional attention. Much concern was expressed about the ways in which new technologies seemed to threaten the humane patient-provider relationship fundamental to traditional health care. One solution would be to ensure that students entering the health professions were trained in the humanistic, ethical, social, historical, and economic dimensions of health care.

The fourth generative influence at Stony Brook was extraordinary. The task of organizing and realizing the new Health Sciences Center on Long Island was given in 1966 to Edmund Pellegrino, who was appointed both dean of the proposed school of medicine and vice president of the yet-to-be-built health sciences center. Dr. Pellegrino was (and remains) an ardent spokesman for what were then new trends in health care education: interprofessional and interdisciplinary training (Pellegrino 1972b). Dr. Pellegrino established a Division of Social Sciences and Humanities in Medicine housed in his own vice president's office. This group was expected to teach courses in and across all five schools of the Health Sciences Center. The division included an historian, a philosopher/lawyer, a political scientist, a sociologist, an anthropologist, and an economist, each with an academic appointment in the appropriate department in the College of Arts and Sciences.

By the time the five schools admitted their first classes in the early 1970s, courses had been planned that were open to all HSC students. Most were required. Some had a clinical focus, such as provider-patient communication. Others, like pharmacology or anatomy, were scientific. Yet others dealt with ethics or social aspects of health care and health care delivery. This last group of courses often combined a number of intellectual disciplines; some were team taught. The most notable were taught on Wednesday afternoons, a time left free for interdis-

---

*In this paper, "interprofessional" refers to the integration of students and faculty trained in various fields of health care. "Interdisciplinary" refers to the integration of the methods and concerns of the various academic disciplines associated with the arts, humanities, and social sciences into the traditionally science-based health care curricula.

ciplinary instruction in all five of the schools. As a result, many of these courses were interprofessional, designed for trainees in all the different professional disciplines represented by our student body.

These interprofessional and interdisciplinary courses were successful both intellectually and socially. Student feedback was favorable. Faculty were satisfied that students adequately met the objectives of the courses. Both faculty and students from across the five schools met and worked collaboratively. Nonetheless, by the end of the decade, interprofessional courses available to, much less required of, students from all five HSC schools had largely disappeared. A few courses taught for some students across two or three schools remained, but the grand project had greatly diminished. Why? What lessons from the past have we brought to our current efforts?

INITIAL BARRIERS TO SUCCESS

DeWitt Baldwin has probably written and lectured most insightfully about the threats to interprofessional education. In an address he gave to our faculty this year on the national experience with interprofessional education, he listed most of the forces that led to the remarkable diminution of our efforts at Stony Brook in the late 70s. Those forces include variations in student preparation and maturity; insufficient experience among the faculty in teaching interdisciplinary and interprofessional work; insufficient clinical experiences and sites for students to be together and to learn to work together; a lack of interdisciplinary clinical role models and of opportunities for students to see a team of faculty working together to thrash out their differences; and resistance (by students and faculty) to new philosophies of education. Perhaps most important, though, were institutional barriers to interprofessional education. These barriers included the school or departmental organization; the academic reward structure; the geographical separation of campuses; differing academic calendars and requirements; lack of leadership in administrative support; lack of physical and faculty resources; and turf issues over each profession's particular scope of practice (Baldwin 1998).

These factors did not all apply with equal measure to our experience in the 70s, and those that did were played out in the context of our particular circumstances. Describing the local influence of many of them would take us too far afield. Two factors, however, are worthy of special note, in part because they played such a crucial role in the 1970s, and because we have discovered parallel perils at work today. They are (1) structural resistance to new programs, and (2) limits on faculty resources. In their own ways, each contributes to a reluctance to make the changes in requirements and scheduling needed to facilitate cross-school curricula.

The SOM faculty had difficulty accepting the three-year curriculum. The initial response to this challenge came in the form of longer days, longer academic years, and covering the material more quickly. Attempts to streamline the traditional curriculum soon succumbed to the faculty's sincere belief that essential material was not being adequately covered. Even the move to four years in the mid 70s did little to diminish that concern, one that still manifests itself today at our (and almost every other) medical school. In this intellectual environment, keeping Wednesday afternoons sacrosanct for courses open and pertinent to students from all of the schools was impossible. One of the first inroads was the introduction into that time slot of an elective pharmacology course, the only pharmacology offering available to the medical students. Needless to say, few of the students felt confident enough to substitute a competing course for this obviously important, obviously clinically relevant one, and attendance of medical students at the interprofessional courses plummeted.

If time for interprofessional training was scarce, so was money. In the late 70s, a seemingly endless state budget crisis in New York devastated financial support for higher education, with serious repercussions for the interprofessional and interdisciplinary programs at Stony Brook. Some HSC schools responded to the crisis by closing programs. The choice of which programs to close was significant. HTM discontinued both its excellent graduate program in hospital administration and its undergraduate program in health education. Other schools cut faculty or faculty time. SSW reduced most of its faculty appointments from twelve to ten months, with a concomitant diminution of faculty availability.

Dr. Pellegrino had left the institution in 1973, and his joint position was split. Dr. Howard Oaks moved from the dental school to become vice president for health sciences, and Dr. Marvin Kuschner was appointed dean of the School of Medicine. The Division of Social Sciences and Humanities was halved from six to three faculty salary lines. More important, it was moved out of the vice president's office, where it had symbolically been a part of all five schools, into the School of Medicine where Dean Kuschner believed he could better protect its mission. When faculty resources became scarce, the focus of their work inevitably became more localized within SOM.

Although problems with scheduling, standards, institutional support, and student diversity weakened interdisciplinary, interprofessional teaching, some areas of collaboration remained. Allied health, nursing, and social welfare continued to offer shared courses for their students. Medical, dental, and, for a while, graduate nursing students also took some courses together, but offerings that included all five HSC schools languished. Because of the political and economic power of the medical school within the institution, any steps toward restoring greater integration would require changes there first. Those changes began at the end of the next decade.

A RETURN TO THE ORIGINAL CONCEPT

Dr. Jordan Cohen's arrival as dean of the medical school in 1988 prompted a review and revamping of the medical school curriculum, aligning it with the recommendations of the report earlier in the decade by the Panel on the General Professional Education of the Physician and College Preparation for Medicine (GPEP 1984). Most important for our discussion was a substantial reduction in the time students were required to spend in formal classroom instruction along with a major re-emphasis on interdisciplinary education, particularly in the social sciences and humanities. For the time being, there were no formal moves toward increased interprofessional education, but the background conditions necessary to make it possible were beginning to reappear.

Dr. Norman Edelman was appointed dean of the School of Medicine and was also named vice president of the Health Sciences Center in 1996, reuniting the two roles divided when Dr. Pellegrino left. It fell to Dr. Edelman to bring back the second element of Stony Brook's early mission: restoring HSC-wide inter-professional training.

There were good reasons why we and others recently turned or returned to interprofessional, interdisciplinary teaching; they parallel those used to justify the efforts made twenty-five years ago. That vice presidents Pellegrino and Edelman expressed their visions in such similar language is evidence of this pattern; once again, "close collaboration" and "working together" had become our maxims. Three significant factors affected both eras.

First, the number and variety of health care providers has continued to increase, making the ability to collaborate with others in practice settings ever more important. The belief was that shared training experiences enable future providers to develop skills in interdisciplinary communication, understanding, and problem solving, even as they learn the particular stances and skills that mark each unique profession.

Second, the increasingly complex organization of the health care delivery system has raised challenges to traditional views regarding scope of practice. As the health care setting has been transformed, cross-training has posed a challenge to specialization. The potential for overlap of responsibilities in health care has steadily increased. Understanding and valuing the training and skills of other kinds of health care workers is essential if these changes and reconfigurations are to occur smoothly.

Third was the belief that familiarity with some subject areas—such as law, ethics, research methodology, communication, and economics, among others—was needed by all health care practitioners. Surgeons, administrators, and lab technicians, for example, all need to know the moral and legal significance of confidentiality and how to evaluate new or alternate methodologies.

For a number of interesting reasons, these same areas of study have been viewed as especially appropriate for interprofessional training.

First, students entering the health professions tend to be equally untutored in these subjects, and this equality of ignorance mitigates the pedagogical difficulties that arise when there are different levels of sophistication in a student population.

Also, because of their explicitly normative content, these subjects are more effectively taught in a setting where students from diverse backgrounds and directions can share perspectives. Integrating students from all five HSC schools provided valuable opportunities for this enriching diversity.

Finally, since most schools already taught this material in one form or another, offering common courses in these subjects would both fit with existing program requirements and offer economies of scale.

These considerations prompted efforts to re-establish HSC-wide interprofessional education. In 1997, Vice President Edelman, with significant help from Lorna McBarnette, then dean of the School of Health Technology and Management, sought funds to facilitate the project. The Josiah Macy, Jr., Foundation awarded funds for the development, presentation, and evaluation of a pilot core course. The challenge became how to use those funds to create a course with intellectual and interpersonal quality, one that would attract students from all five HSC schools and, perhaps most serious, one that would fare better than its predecessors did in the 70s.

FIRST STEPS

How does one create a new course to be taught in several schools at once, with different calendars, administrative rules, and academic requirements? What sort of course would be interesting and accessible to students with different backgrounds and levels of sophistication? The system most likely to succeed would require genuine support from the deans of the five schools and would involve a group of faculty representatives from all schools working together to develop the new offering. The story of that group's work is both a lesson in complex curricular development and, more important, is itself an example of the fruits of effective interprofessional collaboration. The planning of the program was itself a vehicle for building interprofessional relations.

The first step was to get the deans of the schools involved. Dean Edelman (SOM) and Dean McBarnette (HTM), as authors of the grant application, were obviously committed from the outset. The deans of social work and nursing, each of whom had lived through the demise of earlier HSC-wide programs in the 70s, were guardedly supportive. They both encouraged interprofessional and interdisciplinary programs on a smaller scale but were understandably concerned about the continuing existence of hurdles. The dean of the dental school was on the verge of retirement and remained largely uninvolved. His example undermined support from dental school faculty and, thereby, their students.

Each of the deans was asked to select up to five faculty members to serve in a planning group, which Peter Williams was chosen to lead. The deans chose faculty they knew were both exceptional educators and adept at working with other professionals. Williams, a lawyer and philosopher, was chosen for several reasons: He is the head of the Division of Medicine in Society, the progeny of the old Division of Social Sciences and Humanities in Medicine; he had extensive experience running and being involved in interdisciplinary courses; and he had long had contact with the faculty in all five schools. In the presence of the deans, whose support remained essential, Vice President Edelman charged the faculty planning group at its first meeting in January 1998.

It was clear to everyone that some immediate consensus, if only on the easy issues, was important, and in less than a half-hour the planning group had agreed on five core topic areas that would be covered whatever the ultimate course structure.

- Ethical aspects of health care
- Legal aspects of health care
- Interprofessional communications and counseling
- Health policy and health care delivery
- Research methods and evaluation of literature

A small task force, consisting of a faculty member from each school for each of the topics, was given the responsibility of determining particular objectives, generating a list of readings, gathering other course materials (cases, computer programs, etc.), organizing class periods and assignments, and establishing a method of evaluation to determine whether their objectives had been met.

To help guide the task force's efforts, the planning group developed a list of guiding principles on designing the classes.

- The material should have practical (clinical) application.

86

- There should be clear intellectual ties across the component classes of the course.
- Learning should be active and targeted toward adults.
- Computer-assisted instruction should be used whenever possible.
- The teaching, as well as the material, should be thoroughly interprofessional.

One of the first areas of disagreement concerned the overall configuration of the course. Initially, the planning group favored a rather traditional format: a sequence of modules on the five separate subject areas. There was debate regarding the focus of these modules: Should we organize the course around traditional topics (law, then ethics, then research...) or around professions (nursing, then medicine, then social work, then...) or around a local problem or program (cancer, or elder care, or contamination of ground water, or...)? Some faculty argued that the goals of the course would best be achieved, not in a classroom experience, but in the clinic or community. Students would more readily abandon old stereotypes while working away from the locus in which those stereotypes were most firmly, if tacitly, embedded—the Health Sciences Center itself.

The curse of having twenty-plus hand-picked pedagogues on a planning committee was the surfeit of incompatible, yet creative and workable, ideas. The blessing was their ability to listen and, in this case, work to reach consensus. Like so many fruitful debates among reciprocally respectful colleagues, the sides in this deliberation appreciated the merit of the others' positions, and the discourse became progressively more collaborative. The first hurdle—indecisiveness—was surmounted largely because the deans had chosen faculty they knew could model interprofessional collaboration.

We ultimately settled on a format, deciding that interprofessional communication was the essential starting point, and that this core topic area would receive immediate attention. We also concluded that holding the initial class meeting off campus and for an extended period of time would facilitate the building of relationships. The planning group believed that the introduction of the other four topics would best be done in a more traditional setting, but the group also considered it important that the students be required to apply, and not just recall, the subject matter, and that they be given the opportunity to collaborate in interprofessional student groups independent of faculty. The course was structured so that the students would need to rely on each other to succeed. We decided that the students in this first course would all be graduate students, both to minimize the disparities in background education and to permit the pedagogical latitude possible when teaching adults.

As a result, we determined that the pilot course would include three kinds of learning experience.

- All-day get-togethers, held off campus to increase the likelihood that students would develop interpersonal and interprofessional relationships. The core topic, interprofessional communication, would be emphasized.
- A set of classes introducing four substantive topics—ethics, law, policy, and research—in which students would be given the content and tools they would need for the final element of the course.
- Independent (although mentored) collaborative projects by interprofessional groups of students.

The final schedule reflected all of these elements. The semester-long course would begin and end with all-day retreats at a conference facility not far from the Health Sciences Center. The opening retreat, organized by the faculty group responsible for the communication curriculum, stressed collegiality and interdependence. Four more traditional classes followed, each providing baseline information regarding the four substantive foci. These topic classes would serve to transfer a core of information important for all health professionals. More important, these classes were designed to ensure that all of the students shared a common intellectual background, not just the common experience of learning a body of material together, but a common language and understanding on which they could rely when defining and completing their projects.

Then six weeks would be spent on mentored collaborative projects by student teams, each working on an issue related to one of five areas: chronic illness, migrant workers, alternative medicine, scope of professional practice, and international health.

These projects were designed as the vehicles through which the students would practice learning and working together. The faculty and project groups would determine the questions asked as part of the projects; the reports would require the students to apply, not just talk about, their research. At the last, day-long retreat, students would report back to the whole group on their projects.

FIRST STUMBLES

Not surprisingly, problems arose as the faculty worked to turn this idea into an actual course. Each step involved a great deal of discussion, requiring the group to adopt different problem-solving strategies. Some of the problems were solved; others remained and were simply not allowed to frustrate the process.

Important examples of problems concerning administration, personnel, and students follow.

Administrative Adversity

First, there were the anticipated administrative hurdles. No provision existed in the registrar's office for a course allowing credit to students from all five HSC schools. The HSC course designation had to be established in order to create this first core course, HSC 500: "Health, Sciences, and Society."

Scheduling, the second issue, was more problematic. Each of the five schools has an intense and carefully integrated curriculum, working according to its own scheduling system. Some schools teach over semesters; others don't. Some schools do all of their classroom teaching during the day; others run their graduate courses only in the evening. Many clinical schedules make students sporadically available, if at all, on any given day. Especially troubling for us was dentistry, where students are so heavily committed to required classes or clinics that they can't be extracted at any time of day. Some schools have weekend classes; for others, weekend classes are anathema. Even the scheduling debates within the schools were complicated.

A third issue concerned grading and credit for the students. Some schools always assign letter grades to their students; some permit pass/fail evaluations; one accepts honors as well as pass or fail. We decided to assign grades and let individual schools translate these as they wished.

To date, we have been able to avoid confronting the dilemmas of full-time equivalents, responsibilities, and rewards for the faculty. As seen below in the evaluation discussion, faculty still feel sufficiently rewarded by participation with each other in this remarkable pilot project. But none of us expect that enthusiasm to remain undiminished.

None of these administrative difficulties has been entirely intractable. What was necessary was a commitment and act of will by decision makers in the participating units—the schools, departments, and programs. It was they who had to facilitate the structural changes by whatever process governed their internal choices. At Stony Brook a good deal of authority, de facto if not always de jure, rested with the deans. So it was to them that we turned when the planning group could not reach a consensus or, although in agreement, couldn't effect the change on which we had agreed. On only a single issue—scheduling when the course would be taught—was the planning group unable to reach accord, and eventually it was necessary for the deans to stipulate that the course would be taught on a Tuesday evening. This rendered disagreement within the planning group otiose, and the group turned to the issue of getting students to enroll for the chosen time slot.

Personnel Problems

Even in the planning stage, there were two recurring difficulties involving personnel. First, two of the five deans left the institution, requiring us to renegotiate existing understandings. When an activity requires the cultivation of and commitment from people in positions of authority, changes within those positions can create immense difficulties. We were lucky. In one case the new dean was familiar with and favored the project; in the other, the new dean was more favorable than his predecessor had been.

The second personnel problem was unhappiness about unfairly shared burdens. It was difficult getting busy faculty to participate regularly in the planning process. As one might imagine, those chosen by their deans for this innovative project were the same faculty chosen by their deans or colleagues to spearhead many other activities requiring energy and imagination. Because of the increasingly onerous work schedule faced by all clinical faculty in these times of falling reimbursement rates, getting clinicians to participate reliably and regularly was especially difficult. This problem seemed most acute with medical school faculty. Furthermore, faculty from the dental school were conspicuous by their absence. The School of Dental Medicine is geographically separated from the rest of the schools by what seems like the longest half mile in euclidean space. Worse, they were involved in a somewhat tumultuous change of administration, from a dean who did not support the project to one who did but who arrived just as the school was preparing for an accreditation visit. As a result, dental faculty were largely invisible both in the planning and, later, during the course.

Struggles About Students

There were difficulties populating the course: Which students should be solicited and how should they be selected? We decided to leave issues of enrollment to the individual schools, each of which would select ten students to take the course in the spring of 1999. The schools adopted different strategies. SSW, HTM, and SON had open enrollment for graduate students and permitted the course to satisfy program requirements. Oddly, most of the eligible and available nursing students had already filled their distribution requirements, nullifying that incentive. A well-respected individual in SDM solicited volunteers from among his students, but the school gave them no compensatory credit nor relief from any other requirements for taking the new course. SOM allowed students to opt out of the pool from which students were randomly assigned to the course. Twelve of one hundred first-year students asked not to be considered.

Because, but for medical students, the course would be an elective, efforts were made to advertise it. The course description was placed on the Web. Students were also E-mailed announcements of the course and its URL. Although posters and mailbox inserts were used during preregistration, the most effective solicitations were testimonials from the faculty involved in the course. By the time HSC 500 began, there were fifty-one students registered. This included twelve students from SDM; eleven students each from SOM, SSW, and HTM; and a disappointing six from the SON. This situation created the potential problem of an uneven distribution of professions in the project groups, a problem mitigated somewhat by the fact that one SOM student and two HTM students were registered nurses.

Another student-related problem for the planning group was how to evaluate the performance of individual students. We decided they would be evaluated not only for their individual work, using a standard midterm with substantive topical questions, but for their collaborative work as well. A group grade would therefore be given for the projects and reports delivered on the last day of class. Also, since health professionals are universally called upon to evaluate each other in professional settings, we discussed, but eventually did not adopt, the use of peer review in determining grades.

HSC 500: 'HEALTH, SCIENCES, AND SOCIETY'

This first offering of HSC 500 occurred in the spring of 1999. Table 1 shows the course schedule, with a list of the objectives and activities of each session.

Each activity was planned and carried out by an interprofessional group of

HSC 500 Course Description on the Web

This extraordinary course will involve students from all five Health Sciences Center schools: dentistry, health technology & management, medicine, nursing, and social welfare. The course will include study of ethics, law, communication, health policy and research; however the major purpose of the course is to cultivate the interdisciplinary collaboration among professional students that is typical of your work in practice settings. In order to serve these goals, the course has been planned with some unusual structural features.

- It will begin and end with an all-day program off campus.
- There will be only five regular class sessions.
- Teams of students will spend six weeks on an independent project dealing with chronic illness, health care for migrant populations, access to alternative modes of healing, determining scope of professional practice, or issues of international health.
- Faculty from all five HSC schools will teach the course and serve as mentors for the projects.

Health, Sciences & Society has been developed and is supported by a grant from the Macy Foundation. HSC students who wish to enroll in this course should contact their school's spokesperson or Peter Williams, pwilliams@uhmc.sunysb.edu. More information can be found on the Web at http://www.umc.sunysb.edu/som/core-course/.

Table 1
HSC 500 Course Schedule

1/26
Tuesday
5-7 pm

Introductory Class: An introduction of and by the deans with an explanation of the objectives and structure of the course.

Administration of the pretest.
Overall course objectives presented:
a) Describe the U.S. health care delivery system and the interrelationship among the health professions within that system.

b) Describe the reasons for and benefits of interprofessional collaboration.

c) Describe the hurdles to interprofessional collaboration and strategies for overcoming them.

d) Describe the roles, values, strengths and limits characteristic of your profession and those of other health professions with whom you are called upon to work.

e) Collaborate with students from other HSC schools in designing, completing and presenting a project that addresses a health care problem.

1/30
Saturday
All Day

Opening Retreat at the Setauket Neighborhood House

Comedy team: an hour-long performance by a professional comedy group, most of whom are health care professionals.

Workshops—interdependence; collaborative problem solving.

Objectives:
a) Students will be able to identify at least four basic characteristics in interpersonal communication.

b) Students will be able to identify four basic components of group process.

c) Students will be able to identify at least three elements of communication pathways.

d) Students will be able to list and describe at least four roles occupied by members of a group.

4 topic classes, each to include up to an hour of didactic presentation and then discussions of problem cases in small, interprofessional groups.

2/2
Tuesday
5-8 pm

• Ethics Core

Objectives:
a) Identify and clarify ethical issues in a wide variety of health related situations—clinical as well as institutional, individual as well as collective.

b) Recount and explain basic ethical principles as they apply to health care situations.

c) Relate ethical principles and reasoning to important law-court decisions, legislation and regulations.

d) Identify and use the perspectives of your own and of other health care professions in health care decision making.

e) Identify and use the perspectives of your own and other cultures in health care decision making.

f) Describe and use listening, responding, negotiating and reasoning skills in addressing ethical questions in health care.

2/9
Tuesday
5-8 pm

• Health Policy Core

Objectives:
a) Students will be able to describe four basic criteria for the delivery of health care in the U.S.

b) Students will be able to define "scope of practice."

c) Students will be able to identify three aspects of scope of practice that impact on health care delivery.

	d) Students will be able to identify two strategies used in an interdisciplinary model for successful delivery of health care.

2/16
Tuesday
5-8 pm

• **Law Core**
Objectives:
a) Students will be able to list the four elements necessary to establish a cause of action in tort.

b) Students will be able to define "informed consent," and describe the role of the Health Care Team in providing a patient informed consent.

c) Students will be able to define "standard of care" and list three sources of "standards."

2/23
Tuesday
5-8 pm

• **Research Methods Core**
Objectives:
a) Students will be able to describe the role of research.

b) Students will be able to identify different types of research.

c) Students will be able to compare and contrast research designs.

d) Students will be able to formulate a researchable problem in focus groups.

3/2
Tuesday
5-6+ pm

Midterm, midcourse evaluation and project group meetings.

March 2–
April 17

Projects interdisciplinary teams studying
a) An issue relating to a group with a chronic condition with a focus on prostate cancer.

b) An issue relating to access to health care by seasonal and/or migrant population.

c) An issue relating to access to alternative/complementary therapy.

d) An issue relating to availability and scope of practice of a kind of provider.

e) An issue relating to a health care issue comparing its resolution in the United States and other countries.

4/17
Saturday
All Day

Closing All Day Retreat at the Alliance Room in the Melville Library
Post-test
Study Group Presentations:
a) Staging of an education program about prostate cancer—a parody of the TV program, Hollywood Squares.

b) Presentation of a grant application for funding for a clinic in Riverhead, NY, to serve migrant workers.

c) Demonstration of a form of massage therapy with a contemporaneous discussion of issues of funding and access.

d) A debate about a current proposal in front of the NY legislature expanding the scope of practice of nurse practitioners.

e) A mock trial of a liability suit against Texaco for pollution in Peru when Texaco was acting in accord with Peruvian but not U.S. regulations.
Evaluation and review

faculty. Each had assigned and recommended readings. The midterm exam questions were posed and graded by the individual topic faculty. The projects were graded by the mentoring faculty and by the faculty observing the presentations during the final class.

EVALUATION OF THE COURSE

There were a number of ways in which we evaluated HSC 500.* The first kind of measurements looked at the structural elements of the course.

What was the distribution and level of faculty participation? Five faculty had been selected from each school; fifteen of the twenty-five were regularly active, although leadership among the faculty moved from person to person over the course of the year and a half. The dental school faculty were seldom available, and the medical school faculty not much more often. The course director was able to find replacements for absentee medical school faculty but had no comparable success in the dental school.

Faculty loyalties moved in interesting ways. Since the students were distributed evenly through the topic discussion and project groups, professional allegiance was impossible. The faculty's level of attendance and participation demonstrated their involvement with their topics and their project teams. This involvement was somewhat attenuated when the projects began because, in that part of the course, the students were responsible for scheduling and assignments, and they often chose times and tasks convenient for themselves rather than their mentors.

The pattern of student participation was also revelatory. As noted above, there were fifty-one students initially registered for the course. All the medical students were in their first year. Of the eleven students from the School of Social Welfare, seven were first-year graduate students, and the remaining four were second-year graduate students. Ten of the students from Health Technology and Management were graduate students, and one was a first-year undergraduate student. Two were nurses, and one was a practicing anesthesiologist. Of the six nursing students, three were second-year graduate students, two were first-year graduate students, and one was a third-year undergraduate. The twelve students originally registered from the School of Dental Medicine were all in their second year.

Five students from dental medicine were dropped after failing to attend the opening retreat, something we believed essential to the course objectives. The

---

* The evaluation team is led by Dean Frances L. Brisbane of the School of Social Welfare. She is assisted by the following members of her school: Carlos Vidal, Charles Robbins, Shelly Cohen, Diana Filiano, and Robert Marmo.

Table 2
Students Taking HSC 500

School	Number initially registered	Number assigned to projects	Number completing course	Number X/Ξ	Median age
SDM	12	7	2	1/1	24.5
SOM	11	11	11	5/6	23
SSW	11	11	11	9/2	30
HTM	11	11	11	8/3	32
SON	6	6	6	5/1	50
Total	51	46	41	28/13	28

remaining forty-six students were eventually assigned to project groups. However, only two students from the School of Dental Medicine took the midterm and received final grades, although three attended the initial and final retreats and completed all pre- and post-tests. All the students initially registered from the four other schools participated in all course activities. Demographic data are summarized in table 2.

Student learning was measured by pre- and post-tests, which were given to all HSC 500 students and to a control group of students from each of the five schools. Each test consisted of a set of multiple-choice questions: fifteen knowledge-based questions, ten questions assessing attitudes toward a variety of clinical issues, and ten questions regarding job responsibilities of various health care professionals. Another section eliciting more subjective material was given only to class participants. Although the initial study design included faculty participation in the pre- and post-test administration, there were not sufficient faculty from each school participating to be included in the final analysis.

Preliminary Results

Because the course has just ended, the only pre- and post-test results that have been analyzed to date are for the set of multiple-choice, informational questions. Thirty-four of the fifty-one students enrolled in HSC 500 took the pretest, and twenty-eight of the forty-one students enrolled at the end of the course took the post-test. The results reported in table 3 are for the twenty-one students who took both the pre- and post-tests.

The mean score on the fifteen knowledge-based questions improved from 45 percent on the pretest to 62 percent on the post-test. This increase was statistically significant using a t-test for paired samples ($t = 3.5$, $df = 20$, $p < 0.01$). There was also improvement on all but three of the questions and for all but one of the schools.

Table 3
Pre- and Post-Test Results in HSC 500

Question	% correct on pretest	% correct on post-test
1. Which are three basic factors in interpersonal <u>communication</u>?	86	95
2. What is the <u>ethical</u> reason for informed consent?	62	86
3. Which of the following is <u>legally</u> accurate re advance directives in New York?	48	76
4. How does descriptive <u>research</u> differ from experimental research?	29	48
5. Which is a traditional <u>ethical</u> argument for withholding truth from a patient?	14	38
6. Which is not a role of a group member? (communication)	2	57
7. What are elements of group <u>communication</u> pathways?	10	24
8. What is the <u>legal</u> standard of proof in malpractice cases?	14	24
9. What is the definition of experimental research?	62	76
10. Can an HMO in NY be held liable for medical malpractice?	24	91
11. Scope of practice includes which of the following? (health policy/law)	48	48
12. What are the elements of a successful <u>law</u> suit re failure to obtain adequate consent?	14	48
13. Which of the following <u>policy</u> claims is true re scope of practice?	33	62
14. Which criterion would be used in analyzing a health care delivery system? (<u>policy</u>)	95	95
15. What is the purpose of nonexperimental <u>research</u>?	71	62

One can only speculate on why student performance remained constant (questions 11 and 14) or declined (questions 6 and 15), but students were most critical of the two topic classes covering health policy and research. The results on the other two analyzed parts of the pre- and post-test (attitudes toward clinical situations and knowledge about other professions) showed no significant change, but for one question: Over the semester, a significant number of students came to believe it is not necessary to have a clear hierarchy within an interdisciplinary team in order for it to function smoothly.

The grades the students received in this course were wondrously high (3.86 average), even for a graduate course. The grades on the midterm examination were more moderate (3.26 average). Obviously, the grades on the projects, subjectively assigned, were extremely high, and the fact that everyone in each group got the same grade flattened out differences. The disparity between course grades and student performance on the information section of the post-test gives us pause, although a new course with unusual curricular elements might easily result in elevated grades.

Student Evaluations

In addition to these measures of what the students had learned, we collected student evaluations of the course at the midcourse point, after the end of the topic classes, and again at the end of the course. The midterm evaluation assessed student satisfaction with the delivery of the five topic areas (communication, ethics, law, health policy, and research) and their overall satisfaction with the course, and requested comments on the strengths of the course and suggestions for improvement. The final evaluation asked about satisfaction, strengths, and suggestions.

The students were generally positive about the course, as was evident from both the quantitative and comments sections of the evaluation form. On a scale from 1 to 9, with 1 indicating disagreement and 9 indicating agreement with positive statements about the course, the median rating for more than three-quarters of the items was 8 or 9. The topics most positively rated were law, communication, and ethics. The most commonly described strengths of the course were enthusiasm, preparedness, communication, and the opportunity to interact with other disciplines. The initial retreat was particularly well received.

The most common recommendations for improvement were to emphasize the various responsibilities of the different health care professions; to change the evening lecture schedule; and to make sure all the disciplines are represented in material presented in lectures. Overall comments emphasized the importance of continuing and/or expanding this course in the future.

In both the midterm evaluation and the post-test, students were given the opportunity to comment about their experiences in the course, as well as to provide suggestions for future offerings. In general, they offered positive remarks, although several criticisms did surface. The majority of those who compared the delivery of the course with their initial expectations indicated that their expectations were met and, in many ways, were exceeded. The group project was a positive focus of these comments. Some students, however, primarily those from the schools of medicine and nursing, indicated that they had expected to gain more insight into other professions. The comments overwhelmingly identified the group project and the interaction with students from the various schools as the best aspects of the course. Students also praised the retreats—primarily the first one—and they expressed appreciation for being exposed to a variety of issues and a diverse faculty.

Several recommendations focused on time constraints. Some students indicated that the time allotted for lectures was insufficient to cover pertinent material. Quite a few indicated that they could have used more time for the group project. Several also specified that students should be able to choose their own projects, with group work beginning at the onset of the course.

A few aspects of the course appeared to need further clarification. A common concern among students was that they were unclear about the grading criteria, especially with respect to the midterm. Some expressed concern that the project grade—a single grade for all members of the group—unfairly benefited students who had not done their share on the project. Some also were unsure about the nature of the faculty's role in the course. With respect to the actual course content, several students emphasized that, despite the objectives of the course, they still were unclear about the scope of practice for some of the disciplines.

Faculty Feedback

Throughout the planning year, during the course, and after it ended, faculty feedback was solicited regularly. The faculty consistently looked for the chance to interact with colleagues from different schools and the opportunity to participate in an experimental and innovative course most valuable. They found most frustrating the uneven or, in some cases, the absence of contributions from some schools and some individuals. In their most recent discussion, as planning is beginning for the next offering in spring 2000, faculty expressed concern with maintaining the remarkable level of enthusiasm and commitment that has marked this first effort. The faculty shared the students' concern about the ambiguity of their individual responsibility in the course (i.e., who was in charge of what) and the complexity involved in coordinating the activities of so many faculty.

LESSONS

With HSC 500, Stony Brook has begun its second generation of HSC-wide interprofessional, interdisciplinary education. It is appropriate to ask whether one can expect the long-term outcome of this program to differ from that of its first iteration in the 70s.

HSC 500 was a success by almost any measure. Faculty collaboration was first-rate, and collegial relationships were begun (or renewed) that will continue beyond and outside this course. Students who took the course were so pleased with it that many have asked for a sequel and/or have asked to help teach the course next time it is offered. Students have begun to attend our planning meetings.

Our enthusiasm about this success must be tempered, however, by the realization that this project has been blessed with three features that will surely change. First, it was supported by external funding that, although not covering supporting faculty salaries, allowed for special activities. Second, the experimental nature and novelty of the course stimulated enthusiasm and curiosity. Third, it was a relatively small, elective course needing to attract only a few students to be viable. For the program to become a durable part of the educational program of Stony Brook's Health Sciences Center, some institutional changes will need to be made.

This pilot course has spotlighted the areas in which our hurdles lie. Not surprisingly they are many of the same that doomed the programs in the 70s and that DeWitt Baldwin catalogued in 1996 as universal challenges to interprofessional education. We were able to avoid some of them this time through foresight and fortuity. A few examples follow.

1. Variation in student preparation and maturity—We chose to limit enrollment to graduate students in each program, and this seemed sufficient to avoid some obvious problems. Most of the graduate programs have students of many ages and with diverse backgrounds, so this problem became inconsequential.

2. Faculty's lack of experience teaching interprofessional work—Almost all of our faculty were experienced with the kind of teaching required. Some were here in the 70s when HSC-wide courses were last taught. This course had no clinical component, obviating the need to include faculty with experience in interdisciplinary practice.

3. Insufficient clinical experiences and sites for students to be together and to learn to work together—To date we have not moved into the clinical setting.

4. The lack of interprofessional clinical role models, of seeing a team of faculty working together to thrash out their differences— The example of interprofessional collaboration by the faculty of HSC 500 was noted and lauded in student feedback. There are areas in the hospital and community where clinicians

work collaboratively and, when we move in this direction, these areas will be our loci.

5. Resistance (by students and faculty) to new philosophies of education—HSC 500 was voluntary and of such small scale that it didn't trigger the immune response of the traditionalists. Fortunately Stony Brook's history of interdisciplinary, and to some extent interprofessional, education will likely attenuate this problem.

6. Institutional barriers (perhaps most important)—Program coordination between schools, particularly scheduling and academic requirements, was the most acute problem. If our five schools are to have a program required of, or even available to, all students, changes will have to be made at all the schools. In the curricula of the Pellegrino-Oaks era, Wednesday afternoons were left open for cross-professional training. The metastasizing medical school curriculum of 1975 was as big a hindrance to success then as the bloated dental school curriculum is today. Time will need to be reserved in the curricula of all the schools.

Similarly, unless there is a sea change in student attitudes, the interprofessional, interdisciplinary course will need to be required or it will remain marginal, taken and enjoyed by the minority of students who appreciate ab initio the value of the course. Another lesson from the past may be relevant here: As long as the teaching of social sciences and humanities in the medical curriculum was a relatively minor component—forty hours in the first year and occasional conferences in later years—students challenged its relevance and relative importance. Dean Cohen increased the course to fifty required hours in both the first and the second years and also markedly increased its role in the clinical years. At that point, students became more accepting. It was clear that this expanded program, "Medicine in Contemporary Society," was, in part, definitive of the mission of our medical school, so choosing to come here constituted a tacit agreement to participate. A required, HSC-wide, interprofessional, interdisciplinary program can expect comparable acceptance.

The other institutional problem we will face has to do with faculty resources and rewards for participating in interprofessional teaching. Interestingly, all of our schools already occasionally share faculty, students, and course offerings with one or two other HSC schools. A number of courses (e.g., anatomy or pharmacology) are taught to students from more than one school, albeit with a single faculty member or a small group of faculty from a single school. Conversely, the "Medicine in Contemporary Society" course draws its faculty from all five schools, although the course is currently only offered to the medical students. HSC 500 combines these models and presents a course taught by faculty and to students from all five schools. The difficulty is that faculty who participate in many of these collaborative, interprofessional programs tend to do so as volunteers, or as an over-load. That will need to change. Schools may elect to hire faculty specially desig-nated for this sort of work, as is the case in the School of Medicine, or in a school that is fundamentally eclectic, like HTM, the schools might expect interprofes-sional teaching from every faculty member.

These changes require an act of will by those in authority. The Macy ini-tiative at Stony Brook has involved the five deans from the outset and, but for the anomaly of the change in SDM, their support has been steady. Some of the deans were here in the 70s when the earlier efforts failed, and they remain wary. Their choices are seriously constrained by the consistent lack of resources that has become chronic in New York. Courses like HSC 500 might be cost effective, an added incentive to make the difficult institutional choices that are required to maintain such courses.

CONCLUSION

We are currently planning the second offering of HSC 500. Virtually all of the active faculty are continuing with the planning process. The new den-tal school dean has promised active involvement from his faculty and students. The elements of the course are going to stay much the same, although some will be rearranged. The projects were considered a success by everyone, as were the day-long retreats. The topic classes will be integrated with the project preparation time to ensure that the discussion of all five topic areas will be tailored more close-ly to the students' concerns.

The administrative issues have been greatly focused and their resolution will depend on negotiations among the deans. Even the more jaded of us are optimistic that they can be successfully resolved. What is best is that this enterprise has already established connections between faculty that will bear fruit for the institu-tion, irrespective of the survival of HSC 500. Interprofessional, interdisciplinary education remains alive and well at Stony Brook among various combinations of our schools. What we are working toward now is a curriculum that spans all five schools simultaneously.

REFERENCES

Baldwin, D.C., Jr. 1996. Some historical notes on interdisciplinary teaching and interprofessional education and practice in health care in the USA. *Journal of Interprofessional Care* 10:173-87.

Baldwin, D.C. 1998. Stages in the development of interdisciplinary and interprofessional education. *Contexts, State University of New York at Stony Brook* (7)2:7-8.

Edelman, N.H. 1998. Cooperative education among the health professions. *Contexts, State University of New York at Stony Brook* (7)2:2.

GPEP (Panel on the General Professional Education of the Physician and College Preparation for Medicine). 1984. *Physicians for the Twenty-first Century: The GPEP Report.* Washington: Association of American Medical Colleges.

Pellegrino, E.G. 1972a. State University of New York at Stony Brook Health Sciences Center. In *Case Histories of Ten New Medical Schools,* V.W. Lippard and E.F. Purcell, eds. New York: Josiah Macy, Jr., Foundation.

———— 1972b. *Education for the Health Care Team.* Washington: National Academy of Sciences.

7

Developing the Interdisciplinary Education Network

Charles O. Cranford, DDS, Yvonne L. Lewis, EdD, James C. Wohlleb, and Harry P. Ward, MD

Two central concerns have driven developments at the University of Arkansas for Medical Sciences (UAMS) since the early 1970s: responding to the public's need for greater availability of medical care and assuring the greatest possible quality of care. Along the way, UAMS has made a significant commitment to the development of educational programs that facilitate the delivery of interdisciplinary education. These programs encompass many community-based clinical education settings, both inpatient and outpatient, and support educational infrastructures on the main campus. The components of this educational continuum provide a network of environments that offers opportunities to bring the knowledge, skills, and expertise of multiple disciplines together in a problem-solving mode.

THE UAMS APPROACH TO INTERDISCIPLINARY EDUCATION

No sooner had UAMS responded to the state's mandate in the 1970s and 1980s to deliver family practitioners and other health professionals directly to small towns around the state, than the institution was confronted with the crises of rising health care costs and the onset of managed care. The shifting environment stimulated changes in the education of health professionals as the styles of practice changed. From solo and small-group practices with relatively high utilization of inpatient care, health care has evolved to large, multidisciplinary practices with relatively high utilization of outpatient services. This shift to outpatient sites requires a greater emphasis on team development than on the physician-as-captain model of previous years.

COMMUNITY-BASED INTERDISCIPLINARY MODELS

The Area Health Education Centers (AHECs) at UAMS have allowed a more rapid movement to a team concept. Established in the early 1970s to address the need for more primary care physicians, by the mid 1980s, the AHECs were turning multidisciplinary training programs into interdisciplinary programs for primary care.

With six principal centers and numerous communities involved in student and medical resident education, this statewide program remains the primary means of extending and decentralizing medical and other health professions education in Arkansas.

The University of Arkansas for Medical Sciences has adopted interdisciplinary education as an institutional goal. The current UAMS six-year plan charges the university and especially the AHEC Program with the responsibility to develop more and improved interdisciplinary education. UAMS is fortunate to have previously established an extensive network of community sites that enhance the teaching of interdisciplinary education. Although the network was established for multiple purposes, a significant purpose is to teach students and medical residents the value, efficiencies, and improvements possible with interdisciplinary teams.

Joining the statewide AHEC Program are two other programs that together comprise the UAMS regional network for education. The Rural Hospital Program began as a UAMS affiliation of five rural hospitals to provide professional and consumer educational programs to these endangered health care providers. Community health centers and community colleges have recently joined the program, and more rural hospitals have been added. Forty members are expected by the end of 1999.

The third program in the network is the distance education/telehealth interactive video program. All members of the Rural Hospital Program are linked to UAMS by interactive video. Also linked are the AHECs and their satellites. The map (figure 1) illustrates the statewide scope of the UAMS regional network. Many community-based educational experiences are available to students within the network.

Developing a successful interdisciplinary education network requires simultaneous efforts within communities and within the academic health center. This

Figure 1
Statewide Regional Network, UAMS

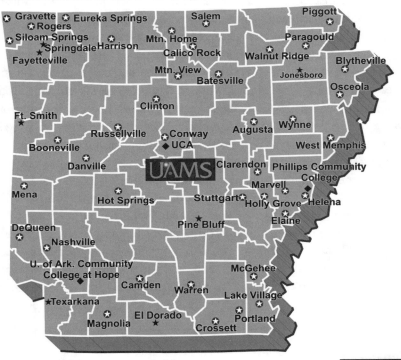

❂ Rural hospitals with compressed video

Augusta - White River Rural Health Center
Batesville - White River Medical Center
Blytheville - Baptist Memorial Hospital
Booneville - Booneville Community Hospital
Calico Rock – Medical Center of Calico Rock
Camden – Ouachita Medical Center
Clarendon – Mid-Delta Community Health Center
Clinton – Ozark Health, Inc.
Conway – Conway Regional Medical Center
Crossett – Ashley County Medical Center
Danville – Chambers Memorial Hospital
DeQueen – DeQueen Regional Medical Center
Elaine – Rural Health Clinic
Eureka Springs – Eureka Springs Hospital
Gravette – Gravette Medical Center Hospital
Harrison – North Arkansas Regional Medical Center
Helena – Helena Regional Medical Center
Holly Grove – Mid-Delta Community Health Center
Hot Springs – St. Joseph's Regional Health Center
Lake Village – Chicot Memorial Hospital

Magnolia – Magnolia Hospital
Marvell – Marvell Medical Center
McGehee – McGehee-Desha County Hospital
Mena – Mena Medical Center
Mtn. Home – Baxter County Regional Hospital
Mtn. View – Stone County Medical Center
Nashville – Howard Memorial Hospital
Osceola – Baptist Memorial Hospital
Paragould – Arkansas Methodist Hospital
Piggott – Piggott Community Hospital
Portland – Portland Community Health Center
Rogers – St. Mary-Rogers Memorial Hospital
Russellville – St. Mary's Regional Medical Center
Salem – Fulton County Hospital
Siloam Springs – Siloam Springs Memorial Hospital
Stuttgart – Stuttgart Regional Medical Center
Walnut Ridge – Lawrence Memorial Hospital
Warren – Bradley County Medical Center
West Memphis – Crittenden Memorial Hospital
Wynne – Cross County Hospital

★ AHEC

◆ Colleges/
Universities

paper describes both the community-based interdisciplinary educational experiences for UAMS students and the infrastructure on the main campus that supports them.

The AHEC Program
Twenty-five years of experience demonstrate that the Arkansas AHEC Program

nurtures educational activities across disciplinary lines. The AHEC is an ideal place for encouraging and facilitating involvement of individuals, institutions, and organizations eager to collaborate. It is also a good place to maximize scarce resources. Interdisciplinary team members share leadership roles and work interdependently. They become active members of the team by transcending their discipline-centered identity. The community's increased role in health care becomes more evident as students and professionals appreciate the resources and strengths in each community that can help with intervention, acute care, and chronic care of health problems. The advantages to students who eventually enter practices where they are team members are clear. Although more research is needed to assess the comparative effectiveness of interdisciplinary education in different teaching environments, the team approach is clearly a progressive strategy for education in the late 1990s and on into the next century.

The AHEC Program functions as a two-way communication vehicle, extending the University of Arkansas for Medical Sciences' programs to all areas of the state and providing a channel through which information concerning health needs, problems, and the views of health professionals and the general public can be conveyed to the medical center. Full- and part-time faculty in medicine, nursing, pharmacy, and several health-related professions staff the program. The AHEC centers function as satellites, or miniacademic health centers under the

Table 1
Typical Arkansas AHEC

Governance	Facility/Location	Faculty/Staff	Students/Day
Component of UAMS Director reports to vice chancellor for regional programs Local Advisory Council Staff are university employees	22,000 square feet 2 classrooms; 1 equipped w/ interactive video Family medicine center: 15 exam rooms, 1 procedure room, 2 nursing stations, X ray, lab, EKG & ultrasound City size: 45,000 1–2 affiliated hospitals Serves 12 counties	4.66 full-time, 4 part-time physician faculty 118 volunteer physician faculty 1 full-time PharmD 1 full-time PhD nurse educator 2 allied health faculty (varies per AHEC) 42 support staff	21 family medicine residents 6 medical students 2 nursing students 2 pharmacy students 5 allied health students (varies significantly per AHEC)

direction of a vice chancellor for regional programs. All faculty have appointments within their respective departments of the UAMS colleges.

The AHEC Program is a principal component of the academic health center with strong support from UAMS, the state government, key legislators, civic leaders, and health professionals. Its overall mission is accomplished through a network of participants from the public and private sectors. This network includes family practice residency programs, affiliated teaching hospitals, libraries, ambulatory care centers, advisory councils, foundations, special-purpose health care institutions, community health centers, health departments, private medical practices, volunteer faculty, and preceptors.

The AHECs have fully staffed teaching clinics. Each center has a freestanding family practice residency program. Centers are staffed for pharmacy education, nursing education, medical student education, and the education of health-related professions students in medical technology, radiologic technology, respiratory care, and social work. Support staff includes psychologists, health education specialists, and a full range of medical specialists within the clinical faculty. There are now 130 family practice residents in freestanding residency programs within the six centers in the AHEC Program. A more detailed description of the typical Arkansas AHEC (table 1) based on an average of the six centers currently in operation, follows.

Funding	Patients	Continuing Education	Community Service
State: 34%	81 patients/day	Medicine: 3,847 attendees/year	Preparticipation school physicals
Community support: 21%	Total: 19,638 patients/year	Nursing: 389 attendees/year	Health department clinics
Professional fees: 40%	Some patients consult by interactive video	Pharmacy: 113 attendees/year	Free clinics
Grants: 5%		Allied health: 254 attendees/year	Support groups
			Health screenings
		Consumer education: 341 hours/year of programs delivered by interactive video	Community presentations
			Library serves 9,000 patrons/year

These statewide classrooms have brought academic stimulation to practitioners in communities throughout the state and reduced the isolation of rural-based health professionals. Students benefit from the program by receiving hands-on practical clinical experiences in settings similar to those in which they will ultimately practice. Communities benefit by having a strengthened health care delivery system. Patients benefit through a higher quality of health care, more accessible to a larger segment of the rural population.

Substantial portions of the third and fourth year of medical school are taken in community-based settings within the AHEC Program. These community-based educational programs allow wonderful opportunities for medical students to interact with nursing, pharmacy, and allied health students who are also participating in clinical rotations at these sites.

Communities are excellent settings for interdisciplinary education. Several interdisciplinary models are used. One AHEC model teaches family practice residents to do comprehensive work-ups on geriatric patients and to understand how geriatric patients differ from younger, healthier adults. The patients are usually newly admitted to nursing homes and need comprehensive physical examinations. The clinical team consists of a physician, a pharmacist, a nurse practitioner, a family practice resident, an OB/GYN resident, a social worker, a psychologist, and students from medicine, nursing, and pharmacy. The family practice residents conduct a full work-up of each patient. Pharmacist and physician faculty review the medication lists with the resident, making sure that there is an indication for all of the medications and no duplication of therapy; that the drugs are appropriate for the patient's age, renal function, and disease states; and that there are no adverse reactions or interactions.

The team ensures that all laboratory work ordered is necessary to monitor the patient's drug and disease states. The social worker and psychologist help with social problems and assess mental status. The nurse practitioner assists with a physical examination and orders for laboratory tests. A faculty physician serves as team leader to coordinate all group efforts. Together, the clinical team develops a care plan for the patient that takes into consideration all of the practitioners' different areas of expertise.

A second interdisciplinary training model has been implemented as an integral component of a rural health outreach project called HeartWatch. The project provides clinic services, health education, outreach, and transportation for hypertensive and diabetic patients in an extremely poor, underserved rural county. The core team includes a physician medical director, a registered nurse health educator, an outreach worker, and a counselor. The clinic faculty teach the team approach to family practice residents, medical students, and nursing students who rotate through the clinic or practice there as a second site.

As patients are seen in the clinic, the faculty and residents identify patients with hypertension and diabetes (or patients at risk for those diseases) and refer them to the health educator in the clinic. The health educator teaches the patient how to manage the disease; motivates the patient to make lifestyle changes in nutrition, exercise, smoking cessation, and stress management; and encourages the patient to participate in HeartWatch self-help groups. The outreach worker provides follow-up contacts and appointments for the patient to return to the health educator; assists indigent patients in obtaining free prescription drugs from various pharmaceutical companies; and arranges transportation for medical appointments if needed. The health educator refers the patient to a counselor if social services are needed. The core team communicates orally with each other and through progress notes in the medical record.

A community team of HeartWatch affiliates provides valuable support services that impact patient outcomes. The community team includes the state Department of Human Services, its public health unit, churches, pharmacies, and the County Extension Office.

HeartWatch patient data are entered into a database, and reports are produced that track the progress of individuals. The health educator and outreach worker review the reports to determine which patients need further follow-up and health education.

In a third interdisciplinary model, a multilevel, comprehensive patient education/counseling program has been initiated. The clinical-based program has been designed to be a system of intervention utilizing individualized education prescriptions (IEPs) to refer patients to a patient educator/counselor for services. Either a faculty or resident physician refers patients of the family medical centers to the patient education/counseling program. The clinical counseling team prepared to facilitate behavioral intervention includes nurse practitioners, doctorally prepared pharmacists, health promotion specialists, and clinical psychologists. This comprehensive behavior-based program utilizes interdisciplinary team members to define and match the proper primary, secondary, or tertiary interventions with each patient's health concerns.

The goal of primary patient education is to utilize health information to help patients eliminate or replace high-risk behaviors. More intense counseling services are available for patients who need assistance in designing personal behavior-change plans. In many situations, group counseling services are available for help with specific issues, including smoking cessation and weight management. All of the physicians, pharmacists, nurses, and health promotion specialists are trained by a clinical psychologist to utilize a readiness-to-change algorithm in assessing the appropriate behavioral intervention for each patient.

The patient's physician determines the initial level of intervention, and an appropriate referral is scheduled. Progress notes are recorded in each patient's medical record to ensure that the physician will receive direct feedback from the counselor regarding the successes/failures of the patient's behavior-change initiatives. All patients negotiate a behavior-change contract with the counselor and are mentored and assessed throughout the planned intervention period. Disease management plans, including hyperlipidemia, asthma, hypertension, diabetes, and low back pain, are designed utilizing the expertise of the interdisciplinary team. A doctoral-level pharmacist provides specific input about the medication management of patients to complement behavioral interventions for asthmatics and diabetics.

> *Feedback from each student provides a clearer understanding of the unique contribution that each profession brings to a patient encounter.*

This education/counseling model is designed to take full advantage of the unique talents and skills of a team composed of diverse health professionals. The team functions as a support cast to the physician and patient in helping the patient obtain the best possible health care. The model operates circuitously and, for the patient, begins and continues as a developing relationship with the family practice physician.

Community Health Centers

Partnering between the AHEC Program and community health centers supports interdisciplinary experiences for health professions students in unique community settings in underserved areas. Through fellowship grants from the National Health Service Corps, clinical experiences and structured forums have been created to meet interdisciplinary educational needs. In this model, medical and nursing students from UAMS and social work students from the University of Arkansas at Little Rock participate in interdisciplinary teams of practitioners and students at community health center training sites. All trainees participate in on-site, interdisciplinary patient case reviews and weekly meetings to encourage interaction, promote discussion of patients and community resources, and foster a team approach to patient care. These sessions culminate in a didactic session focusing on interdisciplinary methods using standardized patients.

The students experience patient-interviewing, diagnosis, and case management in a staged clinical setting with UAMS faculty. All students on the team are encouraged to interact with the patient, then to discuss and analyze the experience as it occurred. Feedback from each student provides a clearer understanding of the unique contribution that each profession brings to a patient encounter. In addition to the didactic learning, students are able to identify the individual roles of other team members and develop effective intervention strategies for their patients, based on available community resources.

University Affiliated Program of Arkansas

Another community-based model is the interdisciplinary training provided by the University Affiliated Program (UAP) of Arkansas. This organization, whose primary mission is to support the health care of individuals with disabilities and families of children with disabilities, has developed exemplary interdisciplinary educational experiences for students and practitioners from a variety of disciplines.

One UAP rural interdisciplinary project concentrates on intervention for rural children with disabilities and chronic illnesses. The program provides preservice interdisciplinary training for students from different disciplines working with children with neurodevelopmental and related disabilities, and in-service training for professionals working in these disciplines. Skills gained from UAP training include interdisciplinary teaming, cultural competence, service coordination/case management, and consultation with paraprofessionals, teachers, health aides, and parents. Individuals collaborating in an interdisciplinary model share goals and work interdependently; they share leadership roles and learn that interactions are important because they affect teamwork and outcome.

CAMPUS-BASED INFRASTRUCTURE SUPPORTING INTERDISCIPLINARY EDUCATION

In addition to the AHECs and other community-based learning opportunities with various partners, UAMS has developed a strong and perhaps unique infrastructure to support and enhance such activities. Its components include a clinical skills center, a center on aging, Web-based instruction, faculty skills training, the Inter-Professional Educational Development Task Force, and an affiliation with the Tulane University School of Public Health.

Clinical Skills Center

The clinical skills center functions as a mock clinic with ten fully equipped examination rooms and a central observation room. Each clinic room has two cameras with sound and feedback capabilities. The observation room contains ten viewing stations equipped with color monitors, headsets, VCRs, and a microphone and central control center. The observation area also has a video projector, which allows a large group of students to view the activities from any of the ten clinic rooms.

All colleges at UAMS have the opportunity to use the clinical skills center for student teaching and testing. The center provides a safe and realistic clinic environment for the primary purpose of educating and assessing health care professionals in practical clinical skills such as history-taking, physical examination, patient interaction, and interpersonal communication.

Many of the activities in the clinical skills center utilize "standardized patients," who are actors trained to portray clinical cases consistently for health professions students. Originally, the standardized patient program was established only for medical student education. It has evolved to include interdisciplinary education involving fourth-year pharmacy students with third- and fourth-year medical students. Further interdisciplinary education projects are being considered in which students from all colleges would form teams that would be trained together and tested on their team strength and interaction.

Center on Aging

The UAMS Center on Aging facilitates the development of interdisciplinary education, service, and research in geriatrics through an education advisory committee composed of representatives from all UAMS colleges and the AHEC Program. An outcome of this approach is an interdisciplinary elective course on death and dying offered through the College of Pharmacy.

In an interdisciplinary format, the course prepares students to manage end-of-life care, particularly through exploring personal issues related to mortality, learning a team approach to such care, developing communications skills needed for caregiving, examining ethical issues related to death, and identifying the economic and social aspects of funeral practices. Didactic exercises and directed tutorials are utilized, and discipline-specific readings are assigned. This course fosters intercollegiate and interdisciplinary approaches to learning and prepares health professions students to provide treatment for terminally ill patients. The students have requested that they work with a funeral director and plan a funeral, also.

Web-Based Instruction

WebCT is one of a multitude of Web-based tools available to course designers and instructors with the potential to facilitate interdisciplinary education. At UAMS, instructors are currently using several of the WebCT tools, particularly to post the syllabus, lecture notes, and images that can be easily updated and revised. Another popular feature is the Quiz/Survey function. It has mainly been used for practice quizzes, which can be very effective when enhanced with instructional feedback on incorrect answers. The private E-mail and bulletin-board tools are being used to increase communication between students and between the instructor and students as a group or as individuals.

One of the barriers to traditional interdisciplinary education is the difficulty in scheduling time when faculty and students from different disciplines will be available for interdisciplinary instruction. A Web-based course, by its nature, is not bound by time or place and thus is ideal for solving the scheduling problems of interdisciplinary courses. Also, a Web-based course, and particularly one using WebCT, can provide information rich in visual, verbal, and auditory information, identifying relevant course material that lends itself to an interactive delivery. It is ideal for presenting patient cases that can be discussed from the perspectives of different disciplines and different professions. Cases may be presented using motion video, photos, charts, X rays, sounds, patient records, et cetera.

Lastly, Web-based instruction can be designed to be interactive. Early reports on the use of Web-based courses indicate that teachers experience more questions and feedback from the students in such courses than in their traditional face-to-face teaching. Much of the interaction may be designed as part of the course, but the medium itself reduces the embarrassment of asking questions in front of one's peer group or students from different disciplines.

Improving Faculty Skills

In the discussion of interdisciplinary education, it is important not to forget the need for professional development of faculty who participate in the interdisciplinary model. Two UAMS interdisciplinary programs focus exclusively on filling this need. One is the Teaching Scholars Program, which seeks to improve education at UAMS by improving the educational skills of its faculty. Large- and small-group exercises, guest lectures, and individual presentations are utilized to integrate new information and skills with current teaching practices. All colleges have faculty participating in the Teaching Scholars Program, which encourages interdisciplinary interaction to take place in the learning process.

The second program being offered to UAMS faculty is an interdisciplinary course in palliative/hospice care. Participants attend formal lectures by visiting faculty from medicine, pharmacy, and nursing who are recognized leaders in palliative care. They review a series of palliative-care texts and attend workshops to discuss case-based scenarios that illustrate an interdisciplinary approach to palliative care.

Inter-Professional Educational Development Task Force

To make interdisciplinary education successful, commitment is necessary throughout the institution, and UAMS leadership continues to look for interdisciplinary opportunities. The Inter-Professional Educational Development Task

Force was created in 1998 to assess existing interprofessional educational programs, to determine if there is a need to develop additional activities and to recommend a structure that would enable such development. The task force noted that rotations at the AHECs provided the best environment for further development of interdisciplinary courses. However, the task force stated, training for interdisciplinary teams should involve students at varying levels of academic accomplishment. It is important that students be exposed to the principles of the interdisciplinary learning model prior to their rotation at community-based clinical settings.

To address this concern, a proposal to establish a department of interprofessional studies in the UAMS graduate school is currently under consideration. The UAMS graduate school would provide an academic home for interprofessional studies on the main campus that would bridge current health professions education programs. Faculty teaching interdisciplinary courses would have joint appointments. Possible courses are research design, teaching skills, geriatric therapeutics, alternative medicine, practice management, scientific writing, ethics and professional integrity, health care policy, and economics.

Public Health Education

Lacking a school of public health within the academic health center, an affiliation was established between UAMS and the Tulane University School of Public Health and Tropical Medicine in 1994. The three objectives of the affiliation are to (1) foster joint projects between the two institutions; (2) deliver the master of public health degree program in Arkansas; and (3) recruit public health professionals to the state. One outcome of this affiliation has been to enhance the infrastructure for delivering interdisciplinary education to UAMS students, medical residents, staff, and faculty. As the affiliation matures, there will be opportunities to involve public health professionals in community-based educational settings.

Meanwhile, an "executive model" master of public health degree program has been established. It is in its third year of operation, with thirty-five students currently enrolled. The program caters to employed health professionals by teaching courses on Friday afternoons and Saturdays of alternating weeks. Its thirty-six hours of instruction are integrated into a practical project, usually in the students' places of employment. These projects have produced useful results for employers, health professionals, patients, and the public. With diligence, students can complete the degree within two years. Classes are held on the UAMS campus where students have access to all of the educational resources of the institution. Plans are underway to also deliver the program via interactive video to students at two additional locations within the state. Initiation of the program was assisted by grants from the federal Health Resources and Services Administration (HRSA), W.K. Kellogg Foundation, Entergy Corporation, and the SHARE Foundation. In the current session of the Arkansas General Assembly, the Arkansas Department of Health was authorized, for the first time, to support four employees per year in pursuit of the master degree in public health.

Adding infrastructure to the educational network utilizing the Tulane School of Public Health and Tropical Medicine was accomplished through non-traditional approaches to serving needs in the state of Arkansas. The affiliation is ongoing and enjoys the support of the leadership of both institutions.

The Josiah Macy, Jr., Foundation has recently published a paper encouraging schools of medicine and schools of public health to include in their mission statements a commitment to prepare graduates for the "synergistic practice of medicine in public health." The report further states that "enhanced synergies should become a central theme of all their education, research, health care and health promotion programs." One could add to these statements that accomplishing the above would be a substantial contribution to the interdisciplinary education of health professionals.

CONCLUSION

To address today's rapidly changing health care environment, health professions education must explore new and more effective methods to prepare students for the professions they have chosen. The interdisciplinary model is one of those methods. In a primary care setting, interdisciplinary teams are an effective tool for promoting both prevention and intervention.

Many experts in the health care field are becoming aware that the practice of public health and the practice of traditional medicine need to become more integrated. Interdisciplinary models of education offer a good place to achieve such integration. Where schools of public health do not exist within an academic health center or within the same state, creative models are needed to optimize health status and minimize the burden of disease.

The existence of an extensive distance-learning network enhances the opportunities to bring public health education to many teaching environments. Communications technology can overcome distance and can allow affiliations that could only be dreamed about a few years ago. Opportunities abound for those institutions that wish to cross old barriers and form partnerships that are mutually beneficial.

In the interdisciplinary model, certain advantages are evident for teachers and students. Broader bases of available knowledge and resources are utilized in patient care. Furthermore, treatment outcomes may be improved by challenging norms and values of each discipline contributing to the care of the patient.

Collaboration and cooperation are key factors in the success of community-based programs. Health professionals in communities are often eager to teach. That commitment increases when the efforts promise some future benefit to the community, e.g., a future resident in a local hospital, a future decision by a student from the community to pursue primary care, or a future decision to return to the community to practice. Volunteerism is nurtured through community participation in local advisory boards, agreements with health care organizations, collaboration with local health care educational programs, and participation by faculty in community events.

The regionalization of interdisciplinary education works when it is part of an educational continuum—when communities view themselves as a vital part of the academic health center. Each entity must benefit from such partnerships. Each must be willing to pool its respective resources to achieve educational goals. Interdisciplinary and community-based approaches to education enrich each other.

In summary, patients benefit from the use of interdisciplinary training when the combined skills and resources of the team are brought together for the patient's health. Health professionals gain an appreciation of other disciplines and what they have to offer. The team members become facilitators of the treatment plan and therefore augment the physician's efforts. The team approach is particularly successful in addressing the multifaceted problems and chronic conditions that characterize most health care.

REFERENCES

Education for More Synergistic Practice of Medicine and Public Health. 1998. New York: Josiah Macy, Jr., Foundation.

HRSA Bureau of Health Professions Rural Faculty Preceptor Initiative, Education and Service Linkage. 1993. *Education for Interdisciplinary Rural Health Care: Program Directors' Resource Manual.* Chapel Hill: Office of Educational Development, University of North Carolina.

University of Arkansas for Medical Sciences. 1995. *Six Year Plan: 1995–2001.* Little Rock: UAMS.

Wohlleb, J.C., S.S. Harvey, C.O. Cranford, and A.C. Anderson. 1997. The master of public health program for Arkansas. *Journal of the American Medical Association* 94:155–59.

MEDICAL SCIENCES CAMPUS-UNIVERSITY OF PUERTO RICO

8

Tools for Effective Leadership in the 21st Century

Adolfo Firpo, MD

Multidisciplinarity is the core of the Medical Sciences Campus of the University of Puerto Rico (MSC-UPR). It is so by design—the product of visionary academic and political leaders who obtained the formal authority from the legislature of the Commonwealth of Puerto Rico to establish MSC-UPR through an amendment of the University of Puerto Rico Law on January 20, 1966. The new law allowed the creation of an autonomous campus solely for academic programs in the health professions. The site was to be the grounds adjoining the Medical Center of Puerto Rico, the largest complex of health care facilities for the integrated delivery of tertiary medical care in the island and the Caribbean.

The law also provided for the financial and administrative integration of the Schools of Medicine and Dentistry—previously independent units—in an autonomous campus under one chancellor serving as chief executive and academic officer. The organizational structure was conceptually aligned with the essence of its mission as stated in the law: "creating the health professionals necessary to meet the needs of the Puerto Rican people through research, education and service." Thus was constituted the first academic health center in Puerto Rico.

MSC-UPR was established as a multidisciplinary center of higher education in health, with Schools of Medicine, Dentistry, and Pharmacy; the Graduate School of Biosocial Sciences and Public Health; the College of Health Related Professions; and the School of Nursing.* The medical complex, a dependency of the Department of Health, enjoys fiscal and operational autonomy under the centralized leadership of an executive director, who reports to a Board of Governors (the island's secretary of health presides). The MSC-UPR chancellor is a voting member of the board.

Under commonwealth law, the Department of Health has been held responsible for providing clinical training sites for the academic programs of MSC-UPR, a public institution completely funded by the commonwealth's government.

This paper highlights some of the challenges to institutional leadership at the MSC-UPR in the late 90s from my two perspectives, first as dean of academic affairs (DAA) and later as chancellor. I discuss two developments on campus in the 90s: the university-wide move to Total Quality Management and the MSC–UPR shift from fragmentation of didactic and clinical health professions education to integration and collaboration, including teamwork. I will also examine the concept of convergence and some of the ways in which MSC-UPR's visionary leadership has applied this concept to activities seemingly tangential but nevertheless critical to the mandate of the academic health center.

A CAMPUS NEWCOMER: TOTAL QUALITY MANAGEMENT

With my arrival to MSC-UPR as DAA in 1995, the campuswide Office of Academic Affairs committed to move the institution toward an integrated academic vision and to establish an operational system enabling the realization of the long-standing institutional mission, as articulated by the collective constituency in 1994, to fulfill the 1966 University Law amendment. This posed a major leadership challenge at a public, multidisciplinary institution with a long history of successes and a culture that varied across the different schools, groups, and subgroups.

It was necessary to develop an integrated quality culture as a cornerstone for comprehensive institutional transformation as envisioned and mandated by the new president of the University of Puerto Rico System, Dr. Norman Maldonado, upon his appointment on February 13, 1993. Under his leadership and with his personal involvement and participation, a major initiative was launched to establish a new organizational culture to replace the attitudes and behaviors of the entire organization.

---

* In 1995, the School of Nursing became the last academic unit to become independent, breaking away from the College of Health Related Professions after nearly ten years of struggle for individuality.

All chancellors of autonomous campuses were charged with the responsibility of developing and implementing whatever strategies were considered necessary to elicit a major institutional transformation modifying their respective institutional cultures. At MSC-UPR, this required moving to an integrated quality culture demanding that institutional leaders convince people that the proposed changes would translate into a new prosperity.

Adoption of total quality management (TQM) practices in 1995…became an effective leadership tool for guiding the process of strategic planning and for also affecting the culture of the entire UPR system.

Adoption of total quality management (TQM) practices in 1995 by the medical sciences campus, through its active and vigorous participation in the UPR's strategic planning process, became an effective leadership tool for guiding the process of strategic planning and for also affecting the culture of the entire UPR system. The culmination of the MSC-UPR campus strategic planning process (covering the period 1996-2001) and the process of its dissemination and subsequent efforts for implementation through strategic budgeting and later zero-base budgeting, were the first formal steps toward pursuing an integrated and potentially realizable quality culture.

Institutional resistance to change surfaced early during implementation initiatives from many middle managers, faculty, and labor leaders who felt threatened by the initiative, seeing it as a direct challenge to the very nature of traditional academic thinking, organizational structure, leadership, faculty responsibility, and administrative practices.

Institutional leaders were required to became role models and personally infiltrate TQM principles to all institutional organizational levels to counterbalance this resistance effectively. During this phase, key roles were played by the dean for academic affairs (who operationally acts as vice chancellor of the campus) and the chancellor. With tremendous effort, the message to the institutional community was consistent, persistent, and widely disseminated, proclaiming: "Academic excellence is the responsibility and the result of the commitment of all members of the institution, from the humblest worker to the most prestigious scholar."

The chancellor, the dean of academic affairs (DAA), and all the deans joined in a vigorous leadership effort to encourage trust and respect between all people. The common vision was shared and explained at every possible opportunity in the simplest terms possible, always exhibiting constancy of purpose and what many considered to be creating the ideal image of the organization's future. Participation was encouraged and volunteers were empowered to test and implement their ideas. Gradually, distrust and resistance fronts started to diminish and eventually a manageable level that would allow effective work in some critical areas of the institution started to emerge. Transformation started to become visible and a change for the better was perceived by many members of the campus community.

THE CURRENT TRANSFORMATION
IN HEALTH CARE

TQM was instituted in a time of accelerating domestic and global change, major shifts in economies around the world, rapid adoption of high technology in all endeavors, and practically unlimited access to information on any subject. Faced with an unprecedented transformation in the worlds of work and health science, we determined to create awareness within MSC-UPR of the emergence of a new world order, where knowledge is currency and technology is the driving and delivering force. This effort demanded intense work and close attention to the continuously changing realities of health care and education in the health professions.

The greatest challenge to leadership in the academic health center today is the integration of fragmented institutions and their equally fragmented operations, converting them into efficiently operating wholes capable of spontaneous adaptation to internal and external forces with full economic viability as they fulfill their missions. In such institutions, visionary leadership becomes the guiding principle toward success.

Organizational structures and hierarchies are often the most constraining forces, yet they are a necessary evil. People within organizations are not yet ready to understand open organizational structures, where the establishment and alignment of knowledge teams occur in response to the issues at hand and to the specific organizational needs of the enterprise. These needs continuously change as intelligent institutions learn and evolve, affecting and being affected by all the forces within their spheres of social and economic influence.

THREE BASIC APPROACHES TO COLLABORATION

Teams are the fundamental units of collaborative work. It is a difficult enterprise, demanding both vigorous collaboration and highly specialized professional skills. Active collaboration between members of complex, highly heterogeneous social groups must be energetically promoted, and when team members start to work together, their success must be acknowledged, rewarded, and widely publicized. The added value of their collaboration must be documented and made prominent. The diversity of those who made it possible has to be vigorously and widely acknowledged, and each participant's contribution recognized, no matter how insignificant it might appear. Upper management appreciates teams that make economic contributions to the institution. Team efforts must also be consistent with the institution's value systems; in turn, the institution must respect the value systems of its constituent members.

Multidisciplinarity

Since the present is the only base upon which to build a future, we must consider here some aspects of the organizational structures of today to appreciate their capacity to influence the efforts of effective leadership. The multidisciplinary nature of an academic health center with a clearly established tripartite mission of education, research, and professional service requires consideration in the present environment. The campus is immersed in social, economic, and political forces that are constantly (and often unexpectedly) challenging and redefining institutional strengths and weaknesses. This highly complicated environmental plasticity affects the institution as a whole and its individual members, singly and in the subgroups they constitute, as well as the forged associations with external collaborators.

Although considered the ideal academic health center by some, MSC-UPR, however, had been unable to become a fully integrated operational academic unit. During my tenure at MSC-UPR, a multidisciplinary institution with a long-standing tradition, many viewed the present as full of threats to the well-ingrained and valued concepts of authority that create opportunities to lead. Active and effective collaborations for truly multidisciplinary educational programs had not been occurring, or at least such collaborations were not being widely acknowledged throughout the institution. Mere physical proximity of one school to another appeared insufficient to promote collaborations among those who believed themselves to be dissimilar.

The multidisciplinary health team approach allows and facilitates the contributions of a diverse group of specialists from several disciplines (or subspecialties of a single discipline) toward the appropriate management of a patient—often with a complicated clinical picture or physical or mental condition. Each expert on the team evaluates the case independently (sometimes one summarizes the case for the others), and each one prescribes his or her own recommended course of treatment or intervention. Management of the case incorporates the knowledge and skills of each member's particular professional discipline. Multidisciplinary interventions emerge from integrating all the individualized interventions or treatments a patient receives. And under ideal circumstances, multidisciplinary health teams can yield high quality, cost-effective professional health care. Each expert individually executes the prescribed specific functions under the purview of his or her specialty or profession. When comprehensive plans are produced, they may reflect professional agreement on the prescribed course of actions, but care is implemented in parallel.

Not surprisingly, observing behavioral patterns in professional interactions at MSC-UPR demonstrates that this fragmented, individualized, interventionist approach to clinical care is most pronounced where providers are from distinct professional disciplines, as in the clinical care and wellness management of persons with developmental deficiencies. Active collaboration in multidisciplinary teams of closely related professional disciplines or specialties varies broadly, and is often induced by the institutional or program policies and standards-of-care guidelines.

In many cases, and more often than willingly accepted, a subconscious fear of being considered ignorant when expressing opinions outside one's area of expertise and professional competence leads to overt arrogance and conceit. Experts, for instance, will sometimes exclude themselves from discussions and considerations outside their professional discipline or area of expertise. The capacity for effective communication and interaction within diverse social environments is eventually lost or at least severely hampered.

In such a psychological framework, members of multidisciplinary professional groups coexist in close proximity but fail to realize the true benefit of their common work space. That is, they fail to understand the needs of their patients (the consumers of their expert knowledge and skills). Thus, the specialist's contribution, more frequently than not, is executed within the narrow context of his or her appreciation of the patient's medical problem without recognition of the client's entire picture. Appreciation of how the treatments or interventions of other team members affect specialized care is generally lacking.

Interdisciplinarity

In contrast to the multidisciplinary approach to health team activities, members of an interdisciplinary health team interact with each other before and after their individual interventions with the patient. The group considers and discusses different points of view on the patient's problem and desirable outcomes from therapy. The final diagnosis and prescribed modalities of treatment or management reflect the group's consensus. Each modality of treatment, however, is executed individually and according to the established professional standard for each discipline, specialty, or subspecialty. The group meets frequently to review and discuss treatment outcomes, sharing information extensively. In short, interdisciplinarity encourages group decisions and management plans, but professional services continue to be rendered individually by each specialist.

Transdisciplinarity

Transdisciplinary health teams take the understanding of the patient as a whole person to its conclusion, forging dynamic knowledge systems in the process. As with multidisciplinarity, the entire team executes the clinical evaluation; their evaluation, however, is more longitudinal, oriented toward the process of care and outcomes, and actively incorporates the patient's family into the treatment process. The team continuously analyzes the patient's progress from the perspective of each discipline, but with the aim of formulating a completely integrated approach, where component elements are validated by each discipline's professional standards.

In a radical departure from other modalities of health teamwork, only one care provider in the team assumes the responsibility of implementing the comprehensive management program. The chosen team member receives training in the specific skills required for execution. There is extensive exchange of information and close monitoring of outcomes so that the specific intervention for any particular case is individualized and transcends each individual discipline. In this way, team participants acquire skills related to functions in other professional disciplines and teamwork is integrative. The patient's problem or the clinical situation is approached holistically.

THE CHALLENGE OF EFFECTIVE LEADERSHIP IN MULTIDISCIPLINARY INSTITUTIONS

The agenda at MSC-UPR during the years from 1995 to 1998 was twofold, as follows:

1. To trigger an institution-wide transformation of our collective culture and operations from a multidisciplinary conglomerate of academics, students, employees, and patients into a balanced enterprise of interdisciplinary and transdisciplinary activities, well-controlled and self-adjusting, leading to excellence in all institutional dimensions.

2. To promote effective teamwork across all institutional endeavors, provoking conflicts in critical institutional areas where resolutions bring about change toward specific, predetermined outcomes while minimizing and effectively mitigating distracting conflicts.

This agenda called for visionary leadership—that is, leadership that brings about change conducive to improvement and progress. This rather pragmatic approach distinguishes this function from management and execution, and establishes the fundamental role of the institutional leader. Appropriate change is a displacement into an improved space more propitious for growth and progress within the broader context of society and civilization.

Since an invitation to change is often perceived throughout the institution as a provocation to abandon the familiar and a displacement from the comfort zones to which people have adapted, leadership is almost invariably challenged. The more diverse and long-standing the institution, the more complex and intricate is its culture; the greater the reluctance of the majority of its members to venture into the unknown and unfamiliar; and the greater the resistance to change and to visionary leadership. Only in times of hardship brought by forces beyond the control of the institution are members of most well-set and established organizations reluctantly willing to try the unconventional and the new.

Crosby (1996) is perhaps the best exponent of a pragmatic approach to leadership in the quest for total quality. He indicates four absolute requirements of leadership in business: a well-defined agenda, a personal philosophy, enduring relationships, and worldliness. A more academic approach to leadership is that of Heifetz (1994), who analyzes leadership in the context of behaviors, its motivators, and constraints. He incorporates a moral dimension into the concept of effective leadership.

At MSC-UPR, we forged our own definition of visionary leadership, integrating concepts from both the Crosby and Heifetz approaches and also on our own experience in improving a highly diverse multidisciplinary institution of higher education. We view leadership as "the totality of activities, actions, and decisions—throughout the institution—that bring about change through accomplishments of a higher moral and ethical order that place the organization in readiness for new transformations to become a sustained meaningful and effective contributor to society at large." This view attempts to address issues particular to institutions of higher education and peculiarities of academic environments, especially in public institutions.

At MSC-UPR, our strategy for implementing our agenda included five key steps:

1. Acknowledge and recognize our past accomplishments and the individuality and contribution of each academic and operational unit, focus attention on issues that transcend their individuality, and challenge the institution.

2. Identify the collective concerns of key internal and external stakeholders, establish an inventory of issues considered critical for the largest segment of the community, and take action on those whose resolution are anticipated to have an easily transforming effect on at least one prominent area of the institution.

3. In the process, reflect deeply and try to fully understand the institutional mission as previously conceived by others, and identify and consider the value systems that exist throughout the institution (by individuals and groups, and of those shared by the majority).

4. Identify the institutional conflicts (potential or realized) and select those of potential use to produce a controlled institutional stress to provoke change toward anticipated and desired results.

5. Carefully formulate a clear vision to fulfill the mission through the integration of the workings of the institution. At every possible opportunity, it is important to verbalize and widely expose the vision in easily understandable terms, applying it to concrete examples of the institutional daily life.

Principles of Visionary Leadership

Leadership is manifested at many levels and in every institutional component independent of the established channels of recognized formal authority (Heifetz 1994). To manage institutional conflict effectively, the chief executive of the institution must draw up a blueprint for leadership that is applicable both to him or her and at all levels of the institution.

The following principles are the ones we embodied and instilled in others while exercising leadership at the MSC-UPR.*

1. Be willing to share responsibility, authority, success, and failure. Seek and involve risk-takers and be willing to learn together with them. Openly challenge those that resist and listen to their concerns; keep them in mind at all times and validate them by comparing their concerns with those perceived as—or demonstrated to be—real threats of wider institutional impact.

2. Be as visible as possible at all institutional levels. Listen and be considerate, not just polite. As you become familiar and trusted, do not be afraid to force the issues you hold true to your heart. Work from the top down and from the bottom up, expecting the greatest resistance in the middle tiers of formal authority, where the greatest entanglement of bureaucracy exists.

3. Conceptualize your vision clearly and verbalize it simply in practical, operational terms relevant to and easily understood by everyone. Be consistent and sell it at every opportunity. Invite questions and maintain control of the exchange.

---

* We found this approach most useful in eliciting manageable institutional stress for directed change in the highly culturally diverse—social and academic—communities of the MSC-UPR. The MSC-UPR, as is typical of other academic health centers, has been traditionally dominated and controlled by the particular interests of the School of Medicine; the mere openly expressed support of the concerns of the other academic units was capable of creating sufficient stress to provoke active and visible debate over issues never before considered worth discussing.

4. Have a clear plan of action to address the institutional needs and to establish the order of priorities. Involve everyone, promote discussions, and respond openly to any challenge with equanimity. Be objective and well documented on every issue perceived to be critical to the institutional well-being.

5. Know the finances and frame all actions within monetary allocations for their realization. As actions are implemented, keep informed on progress realized. Demand that all other institutional leaders do the same.

6. Insist on documenting and publicizing achievements and their impact within and outside the institution. Acknowledge the participation of everyone that was involved in the effort. Describe anticipated future development or progress in each particular area and how present accomplishments build toward the planned future.

7. Support new ideas, pay attention to them, invite discussion and analysis in terms of the capabilities of the institution—particularly about the resources required (and available) for their implementation. Recruit support for testing ideas of potential benefit to the broadest population, allocate funding and monitor progress. Invite input from those anticipated most likely to be affected—favorably and adversely—and make adjustments as required, maintaining a positive balance and fairness with utmost objectivity. If possible, let your peers determine alternatives that may apply to the situation at hand.

8. Scrutinize the obvious and search for the unconventional. (Here is where we attained the greatest success in our efforts to institute efficient leadership at the MSC-UPR.)

The Three Missions and More

This paper does not list activities that promote interdisciplinary and transdisciplinary learning on the MSC-UPR campus (although we have encountered many examples). Academic health centers are highly complex institutions embedded within a rapidly transforming environment where the economy and politics play a dominant role and where effective leadership calls for more than a narrow focus on the development, implementation, and execution of academic programs.

Today more than ever before, we must consider the academic health center as the highly complex system it really is. Nonacademic institutional difficulties can be critically important because of their potential impact on the academic process or because of their adverse effect on the institution's academic development and progress. A strike resulting from strained labor relations or improperly trained personnel causing failure to comply with the demands of funding agencies are two obvious examples.

At MSC-UPR, we developed a vision of academic excellence that results from the contributions of the entire institutional community. Custodial staff, clerks, administrators, and all technical and nontechnical personnel contribute to academic excellence, and their contribution is acknowledged and celebrated. The same kind of interdisciplinary and transdisciplinary approaches applied to team learning for students was introduced to administrative issues and in dealings with the leadership of workers' organizations. We have found this approach (after overcoming the progressive stages of team-building) to be rewarding and a source of great personal and professional satisfaction for all involved.

The Power of Shared Objectives

Self-interest is a powerful driving force of human activity expressed in teamwork as well as in individual effort. Throughout institutions it is easy to identify groups (constituted spontaneously or by design) whose members are of diverse professional and social backgrounds yet are able to work harmoniously and often vigorously toward a common purpose.

In multidisciplinary academic institutions there are organizational structures composed of representatives of all its constituent units with prescribed responsibilities toward the greater whole (e.g., the Academic Senate and Administrative Board at MSC-UPR). There are also activities whose success and execution are totally dependent upon the vigorous interaction of teams composed of wide representation of institutional constituencies.

At MSC-UPR, we conceptualized these dynamic institutional activities or compartments as institutional points of multidisciplinary convergence. Institutional points of convergence across different disciplines are strong catalytic agents for a gradual, systematic, controlled institutional cultural transformation into a more fully integrated operation.

The Advantages of Convergence

Convergence takes place among members of a diverse team trying to address an issue considered critical to each group represented. During active convergence, work and deliberations become vigorous and heated, resulting in (or often leading to) transformation of members during debate. When properly managed by competent leadership, convergence interactions in highly diverse groups almost always lead to some transformation of the participants to a more neutral or reflective stance. It is clearly identifiable as that particular moment during a discussion when we suddenly realize that some possibility might exist to address the concerns of the debating parties in a less threatening manner. In addition, the changes in attitude that emerge during active convergence gradually become expressed throughout the entire institution.

The concept of convergence comes from the natural sciences. In biology, it denotes the tendency of unrelated, distinct animal and plant species to evolve similar structural or physiological characteristics under similar environmental conditions—the very essence of transdisciplinary teamwork. In meteorology and oceanography, convergence designates points or spaces where airflow and ocean currents meet, characteristically marked by upwelling (of air) or downwelling (of water), denoting very forceful dynamic interactions.

Thus, we find the concept of convergence in nature most relevant to the interaction of group members whose diversity is reflected in varying perspectives on an issue. Often, we can address difficult and pressing issues by subtle application of convergence dynamics.

At MSC-UPR, we consider points of institutional convergence to be any activity by teams of high diversity where vigorous interactions can potentially occur and where issues (or conflicts) successfully resolved transform the opinions and attitudes of at least some of the participating members. Transdisciplinary health teams are the ultimate expression of convergence in the health disciplines.

SOME EXAMPLES OF CONVERGENCE AT MSC-UPR

The organizational structure of MSC-UPR in 1995 accomplished broad institutional multidisciplinarity across all educational programs in the health professions and their respective specialties and subspecialties. It also provided formal organizational compartments for academic convergence—usually distinct and separate from compartments of administrative and executive convergence (at least at the operational levels).

Formal institutional convergence at MSC-UPR occurs at the three supporting deanships of the campus (Academic Affairs, Student Affairs, and Campus Administration) as well as at the Academic Senate, the Campus Administrative Board, and the General Student Council.

When I was a newly arriving dean, my ability to identify the institutional points of convergence was a powerful resource enabling me to build operational teams and maximize their impact throughout MSC-UPR. Applying my knowledge of convergence to work at the dean's office allowed our leadership to capitalize on the solid multidisciplinarity of MSC-UPR and to make wise capital investments with our limited resources.

My search for points of convergence throughout the campus disclosed them at all levels—whether formally recognized or not—and between students, faculty members, and institutional employees in various mixes. The Campus Chorus, for example, is composed of institutional employees from all academic and administrative units as well as students from different academic disciplines. Another discovery exemplifying the value of examining unconventional activities was the extremely popular Theater of Life model for transdisciplinary learning. Theater of Life had been on campus for more than fifteen years, but the institutional leadership had never formally recognized or endorsed it as a valued academic approach to education across professional disciplines.

Finding points of institutional convergence became a valuable strategy for identifying organizational compartments and activities with a high capacity to promote the formation and support of interdisciplinary and transdisciplinary work teams. It allowed us to address institutional needs across all sectors in a systematic, manageable way.

The Computer Information System
The Academic Senate and the Campus Administrative Board are among the points of convergence at MSC-UPR. Applying the leadership guideline of sharing responsibility, authority, success and failure, we openly challenged Senate members to debate a major capital investment to update the MSC-UPR informatics infrastructure during a formal assembly of the Academic Senate on May 4, 1995, three months after my arrival. Chancellor Jorge Sanchez and I agreed to schedule an open Senatorial debate on this issue while trying to establish priorities among issues critical to the institution. We intended to elicit a response from the faculty representatives about the possibility of committing significant funds to revamping the technological infrastructure of the campus. We also wanted a consensus that this issue was critical enough to unequivocally prevent funding for any other new initiative (regardless of its merit) during the following two to three years. It would also imply and require the active pursuit of additional funds from outside the institution and the participation of all academic units according to the availability of such funds at local, state, and Federal agencies; philanthropies; and other donors. In sum, the effort was to be the dominant focus and purpose of the campus.

To the chancellor's and my surprise, the Senators' immediate reaction to our invitation was to consider it an act of overt cynicism because the need to upgrade our technology was so obvious (and had been for such a long time) that debate was unnecessary. Almost instantly, the entire Academic Senate decided to attack both the chancellor and me (as newly appointed DAA) for what they perceived as malicious insensitivity.

Perhaps because of our surprise, we remained calm. After people had vigorously expressed their most aggressive emotions, the discussions turned toward a call for action and leadership. Consensus emerged on how critically important it was for MSC-UPR to have a solid, modern informatics infrastructure, providing faculty and students both access to the Internet and free exchange of information with peers and colleagues within and beyond the institution. Given all other institutional needs, we considered an obsolete technology infrastructure the biggest threat to the entire community, and we adopted a formal resolution to address it at whatever cost. The resolution set an agenda for immediate action by the chancellor and DAA and for an agreed-on path for further institutional development during our respective administrations.

The Campus Library

Although the library is the most prominent campus component with major potential for academic convergence, it is often taken for granted except by its heavy users and the library staff. The MSC-UPR library became the nucleus for our new infrastructure development project. We felt that this approach would maximize the impact of the investment and make its implementation and progress evident and relevant to all institutional components. The multidisciplinary committee in charge decided to call the project the Health Education Information Resources System (HEIRS) initiative. Academic Senators, representatives from almost every academic unit, library staff, and administrators from all areas participated in the team activities from conceptualization to development, contracting, construction, implementation, and inauguration.

The project was considered the most successful campus initiative in many years and was demonstrable evidence of the intentions of the campus leadership to fulfill its commitment to the Academic Senate and to the institution at large. It also was received as evidence of administrative expertise and competence by the new administrative body. The process from planning to inauguration rapidly progressed through three developmental phases that had been carefully programmed and implemented.

On June 27, 1996, thirteen months after the Senatorial debate, HEIRS was inaugurated. We completely remodeled the circulation desk and the reserve collection facilities of the medical library, updated and expanded the entire library communications network, replaced terminals with personal computers, and established a telecommunication center containing ten personal computers with free Internet access. Such a project had never before been completed in such a short time.

At inauguration, I, as the DAA, read the names of all personnel, including custodial staff, administrators, purchasing agents, and campus security, who contributed to meeting the self-imposed deadline, and the chancellor personally thanked each one. All institutional deans expressed their personal appreciation to the work teams that made the project possible. The director of the library shared some of her personal experiences on the project's impact on library personnel and how they gradually became so involved with the project that it became a very personal concern. Indeed, the library security guard (an employee of an independent private enterprise) became so involved in the project that he started coming to the library during his free time to help paint the facilities.

Frequent visits and walkthroughs by the chancellor and me were welcome events at the library and an opportunity for direct exchange with employees, students, and occasional outside customers. The information center component of the project was officially designated as the HEIRS. HEIRS was felt to be successful throughout the campus and of documented benefit to students, researchers, and clinical care providers of all disciplines. Later, HEIRS became the nucleus for a major international outreach and information exchange with other medical libraries in the Caribbean. This project led to close collaboration with the School of Medicine and Pharmacy of the State University of Haiti, and with the Autonomous University of Santo Domingo Medical School in the Dominican Republic. The MSC-UPR received funding from the National Library of Medicine for further enhancement of its infrastructure. This money enabled us to improve our HEIRS services throughout the Caribbean and to provide access to HEIRS resources for the neighboring public teaching hospitals at the Medical Center, a community hospital in another municipality, and the two community-based primary health care centers. The library's success produced a sense of trust and confidence in the new institutional leadership throughout the entire MSC-UPR.

The Computer Training Center
Another example of an institutional point of convergence is the Computer Training Center. Six weeks after inauguration of the remodeled library facilities and HEIRS, the Computer Training Center initiated its operations. The facility provides two convertible learning environments for up to sixty users, fully equipped with state-of-the-art computer and digital audiovisual equipment.

The Academic Bulletin
Visionary leadership requires an appreciation of the difficulties that people face as they work to retain their individuality and also find their place within an academic health center. While committed to institutional operational integration (not centralization), we emphasized that working together does not constitute a loss of individuality. An appointment to a multidisciplinary team to produce interdisciplinary outcomes is an invitation by the leadership to take part in the search for

lasting solutions from a broader perspective, one that takes into consideration the whole of the institution rather than simply its individual parts. The objective is to address challenging institutional concerns (often of long standing and previously considered unsolvable) and generate innovative strategic approaches to their solutions. Every action, reaction, posture, statement, decision, and opinion of the formal institutional leadership, particularly of the CEO, must reflect this concept. When looking for approaches to strategy implementation, look for the obvious and identify the unconventional.

The preparation of the biannual *Academic Bulletin* of MSC-UPR is an institutional node of convergence that became a useful vehicle to reaffirm the individuality of the separate academic units. Over several years, each academic campus unit had started to produce its own academic bulletin, leading to redundant expenses and effort. The quality varied according to the available monetary resources and to the attention to detail and eye for principles of graphic design of those responsible for the activity in each unit. The dean of academic affairs, responsible for producing the institutional *Academic Bulletin,* called for a unified effort for revision. A meeting with the staff in charge of the activity led to an endless recounting of difficulties always encountered in preparing this document. Academic units were always late in submitting the required materials, which often were incomplete or not properly updated, and the whole activity was considered frustrating and disruptive of the overall operation of the Office of Academic Affairs.

Through the associate dean of academic affairs and the Council for Interaction and Educational Programming (CIEP), over which she presided, all units were notified of the new dean's intention and commitment to produce a new institutional bulletin that would reaffirm the individuality of each academic unit and its contribution to MSC-UPR. Deadlines for submission of the required information and materials were to be firmly enforced and funds were allocated for hiring a professional graphic designer. The staff was to keep CIEP informed on progress at every monthly meeting.

In two working sessions, the professional designer and I agreed upon the final format for the bulletin. After several months, the bulletin was produced in time for the accreditation visit of the newly created Council of Higher Education of Puerto Rico. All stakeholders were satisfied. Success was attributed to the effective collaboration of all representatives and to the hard work of the staff. All were personally congratulated and thanked by the deans and the chancellor. The institutional Academic Bulletin became a source of great pride to the entire deanship of academic affairs and a concrete symbol of effective teamwork. It became a valuable tool of the leadership for selling the vision that effective operational integration does not necessarily lead to loss of individuality.

The personality of each academic unit is amply portrayed while integrating them into the common purpose of the institutional mission (as established in the law that created the institution and also as expressed in the official Campus Mission Statement document approved by the Academic Senate in 1994). The black and gold front cover (the institutional colors) serves as background for the MSC-UPR logo representing the unified institutional identity. On the back cover, a smaller logo is followed by full color logos of each academic unit with its complete name. The contents, organized into seven sections, present a broad view of the organizational structure and how it supports the common institutional purpose. All academic units are presented individually under the heading "Academic Programs," and each corresponding section begins with a cover page displaying the unit's logo and provides a self-contained sub-index.

The *Academic Bulletin* includes a history of the campus, its mission, and the institutional goals as MSC-UPR fulfills its mission. All members of governing bodies of the entire University of Puerto Rico System are named, enforcing the concept that MSC-UPR is a component of a much larger institutional public entity. The publication is illustrated with photographs of students, faculty, and patients engaged in all sorts of activities representative of campus life and conveying the plurality of its composition and a shared purpose.

Institutional Accreditation

There is no institutional purpose more widely shared by all constituents of an academic institution than the accreditation of its programs and of its organization. There is a collective sense of pride that motivates often difficult groups to unite forces to accomplish this goal. Work for the Middle States Association accreditation and progress report was already in progress in 1995 at MSC-UPR, proceeding in parallel to the preparation of the Strategic Plan for Institutional Development, a required activity for accreditation. Multidisciplinary committees were already established and the action plan for most of the related activities required was being implemented.

The dean of academic affairs presides over the Institutional Committee for Strategic Planning and Development (ICSPD), which brings together into a single body the presidents of similar committees in all academic and administrative campus units and reports to the chancellor. By all considerations, it is an ideal institutional node of convergence through which many issues can be addressed to focus the attention of the constituting members above their individual selves. The work of the committee for accreditation and of the ICSPD also became the ideal vehicles to develop and promote a new vision of effective partnership and collaboration throughout MSC-UPR from the leadership perspective of the dean of academic affairs, which had a wide impact in all spheres of institutional activity.

ESTABLISHMENT OF A NEW INSTITUTIONAL CULTURE

Meanwhile, the chancellor and I, together with all the deans, were joined in a vigorous leadership effort to encourage trust and respect between all people. The common vision was shared and explained at every possible opportunity in the simplest terms possible, always exhibiting constancy of purpose and what many considered to be creating the ideal image of the organization's future. Participation was encouraged and volunteers were empowered to test and implement their ideas. Gradually, distrust and resistance started to diminish and eventually a manageable level that would allow effective work in some critical areas of the institution started to emerge. Transformation started to become visible and a change for the better was perceived by many members of the campus community.

To establish a new institutional culture at MSC-UPR required the creation of a social environment fostering informal and honest communication, a sense of community, and a reduction in the anxiety evoked by the transformation process. Several activities were useful to achieve this control of the collective institutional anxiety at MSC-UPR: the Annual Family Day, the Games Day, and the Total Quality Campaign "Dedicated to Excellence, Committed to Quality" that encourages the members of the community to wear the T-shirt of the campaign every Friday. These strategies helped to eliminate barriers between departments and ranking positions, promoting a sense of belonging on the part of all members of the entire community.

A three-day celebration of a Total Quality Fair provided an excellent resource and opportunity to share knowledge, achievements, and experiences among the improvement teams operating on campus and with the public and private sectors. The activity itself became an excellent interdisciplinary forum of tremendous value for validating the discourse about the importance and benefits of integrative work and knowledge sharing. In addition, the Interdepartmental Quality Improvement Teams and each training activity sponsored by the TQM Initiative included a mixed audience from different deanships, offices, departments, programs, disciplines, and positions. These activities gave the participants the opportunity to know what others were doing, their achievements and problems, and how others might help to solve the problems. They allow participants to see the campus as a whole, instead of as islands. All of these educative and social activities are the bases for developing a culture that promotes collaboration among the different professionals and students from different disciplines toward a common direction. Today, resistance to change remains, but is not totally unyielding.

Great efforts were exerted to cultivate the desire and enthusiasm to change and venture into a controlled transformation process, preferably in strategic multidisciplinary partnerships. A commitment to quality was reflected in the leaders' personal attention and intervention on behalf of the most needful organizational processes, and buying into and practicing the gradually emerging new culture.* In mid 1998, institutional policy for quality was formally established in two documents, making it a commitment of the entire leadership of MSC-UPR. It was done in an open ceremony on campus, with the participation of the chancellor and all campus deans. The documents encouraged behaviors promoting the development and expansion of interdisciplinary and integrated institutional practices and proposed to ensure total commitment from senior managers and everyone in the institution to facilitate cultural change and continuous improvement, and to promote the elimination of barriers between departments and disciplines. The chancellor personally signed these documents accompanied by the leadership of campus labor organizations, who also signed the documents.

CONCLUSION

We strongly believe that we are facing the end of an era dominated by individual experts and specialists and the beginning of a massive shift to the reintegration of knowledge, to teamwork, and to collaboration. It is a time of awakening and reckoning with the demands of a complex society—conscious and informed—a society that anticipates a high return on its investments and demands accountability from all those whose services and goods it consumes or supports.

It is impossible to predict whether this concerted effort and process at MSC-UPR will lead to the gradual emergence of a new vision of health professions education. I hope it will, because there is no other greater challenge to the future growth and development of each of the professions and of the nature, qual-

---

* The pressure on me greatly accelerated in March 1997, when I assumed the role of interim chancellor following Chancellor Sanchez's decision to step down. Maintaining momentum and trust became critical as I had to assume leadership roles both as DAA and interim chancellor. In July, I was recommended for the chancellor's position by the university president with wide support of the campus community and was endorsed by the Board of Regents of the UPR System. Even as chancellor, I continued as DAA until early 1998, when a new DAA was appointed.

ity, and processes for providing care to our diverse societies. True leadership requires vision with a real sense of objectivity about the changes rapidly transforming civilization as we know it. The rules of the past are no longer valid and no emergent solution can guarantee a sustained growth in any sphere of natural activity. Business is rapidly evolving within this new conceptual framework where even the very nature and characteristics of change are changing. It is up to us to meet the challenges head-on and search for new and creative approaches to address them effectively within the framework of the emergent knowledge economy and digital reality.

ACKNOWLEDGMENT

The assistance and support of Dr. Wanda Altreche, director of the Office of Institutional and Academic Research, University of Puerto Rico, is gratefully acknowledged.

WORK CITED

Crosby, P. 1996. *The Absolutes of Leadership*. San Francisco: Jossey-Bass.

Heifetz, R.A. 1994. *Leadership Without Easy Answers*. Cambridge, MA: Belkman Press of Harvard University Press.

9

Embracing the Barriers: An Emerging Model

M. David Low, MD, PhD, Judith Booker, MEd, and Linda Brannon, MEd

The University of Texas-Houston (UT-Houston) Health Science Center is the largest health sciences university in Texas. Established twenty-five years ago, it is made up of a school of medicine, a school of public health, a school of dentistry, a school of nursing, a graduate school of biomedical sciences, and a school of allied health sciences as well as numerous centers and institutes. The UT System created the center by combining formerly independent health-related entities in Houston with an administrative component. Since then, there has been significant growth in all areas of the university; there has also been a continuously challenging effort to create a unified university community with our varied academic cultures and geographically dispersed components.

In this paper we describe a recent major, university-wide effort—still ongoing—to explore our ability and, ultimately, our level of commitment for implementing what has consistently been accepted as an area of great strength and potential: interdisciplinary health professions education. We discuss why and how we conceived this project. We provide descriptions of interdisciplinary efforts we have launched in this decade. We share details about how we have designed and have implemented the feasibility project. Note, however, that as we go to press, the observations we make in this paper about project design and implementation are preliminary, and advice and suggestions to others who might contemplate such an effort are based on personal perspectives and anecdotal information. However, we can already state with assurance that this project—no matter the eventual outcome—has already positively affected intrauniversity relationships and, if nothing else, will stimulate more interdisciplinary collaboration.

SETTING STRATEGIC DIRECTIONS

Since the early 1990s when UT-Houston's leaders initiated an innovative approach to strategic planning, UT-Houston has focused on a vision of becoming a model health sciences university. This aspiration is grounded in a comprehensive assessment of all university programs and an analysis of where our strategic advantages lie. We have used this vision and a renewed mission as a guide for policy and program development, strategic planning, priority setting, and resource allocation. Faculty, staff, students, and community supporters participate in a continuing dialogue about who we are; what we contribute to our community and our state; what makes us unique among academic health centers in Texas; and what we aspire to be in the future.

Facing a budget shortfall in 1991, leaders of the university used adversity to force much-needed institutional change through revitalized and innovative strategic planning. Rather than compel all units to make across-the-board budget reductions, we chose a strategic approach to program review and relative priorities, making dramatic reallocations from lower priority programs to higher priority programs. (Higher priority programs were those deemed to be of strategic importance.)

The initial steps, which we call our "strategic directions," toward becoming a model health sciences university were as follows:

- Evolving into a graduate-level institution
- Consolidating basic sciences instruction
- Enhancing the quality of students
- Transforming dental education
- Enhancing graduate training
- Emphasizing community-based education, training, and service
- Establishing a core interdisciplinary curriculum for all health professions students.

The First Interdisciplinary Course

The aspiration to create an innovative, coordinated, interdisciplinary teaching program that involved all of the university's health professions programs in a health care team approach led to the formation of a task force in 1993 of faculty, students, and administrators. The initial charge was to develop a design for one or more core curricula for all UT-Houston students. Over two years, the Core Curriculum Task Force grappled with many of the issues that remain challenges today. The Task Force reviewed critiques of the education for the health professions, examined the curriculum of each UT-Houston school and areas for possible collaboration between the schools, and defined the obstacles that would impede implementation of the health sciences school concept. In its final analysis, the Task Force concluded that the concept had merit but was impossible to implement in full; instead they proposed the development of an experimental, elective course.

Facing a budget shortfall in 1991, leaders of the university used adversity to force much-needed institutional change through revitalized and innovative strategic planning.

Pilot testing of this prototype would help the university assess the viability of the concept and the efficacy of the instructional strategy. If the course met the expectations of the faculty and students, it would continue to be offered as an elective, open to every UT-Houston student with the permission of the academic advisor.

The Core Curriculum Task Force assumed responsibility for developing the course, soliciting faculty, and recruiting students. Funding for course delivery was made available; however, faculty time allocation was on a volunteer basis.

The first interdisciplinary course was offered during the spring and fall of 1995 as an elective course to second- and third-year students from each of the UT-Houston schools. Because of different academic calendars and other scheduling conflicts, students met for two hours, once a week, in the evening. As an incentive to participate, students received scholarships to cover the cost of tuition, dinner, and free parking.

Because of different academic requirements in the schools, public health, allied health, nursing, and biomedical sciences students received two semester credit hours for completing the course. Medical and dental students received only extracurricular recognition.

The faculty developers structured the course as problem based with teams of students representing varying disciplines. The process was student centered, that is, the students determined the focus of what was learned and how it was applied to case studies.

Volunteer faculty served not as teachers but as team facilitators. To develop a plan for managing a case, the teams were presented with information about hypothetical or real-life case studies over a three-week period and asked to identify problems that would need resolution. Each case study was designed to achieve a number of learning objectives known to the faculty facilitator but not to the students. At the end of this period, the students were informed of the learning objectives of the case, asked to determine the extent to which they had been accomplished, and asked to establish a final management plan.

An evaluation instrument was designed to determine the following:
1. Student perceptions of the course and the faculty facilitator;
2. The facilitator's perception of the students; and
3. Student accomplishment of the learning objectives.

At the end of the pilot study, evaluations by faculty and students supported continuing the course as an elective.

The basic approach and format of this first core curriculum course is still in use. During the past four years, the course, now entitled "Frontiers in Interdisciplinary Health Care," has averaged an enrollment of approximately thirty students per semester.

Although evaluations have shown that the course has been successful and the students consider it worthwhile, the course has not been adopted by the schools as essential to the curriculum. It remains an elective. It is not consistently listed in school catalogs nor is there a common course number across campus. Some students get academic credit upon course completion while others do not. Faculty are recruited as volunteers, and they depend heavily on word-of-mouth to market the course.

The "Frontiers" course has been expanded in various ways in an effort to increase visibility and student and faculty participation as well as expand its scope. Students from complementary disciplines (e.g., pharmacy, optometry, and social work) from neighboring institutions were invited and have enrolled in the course. At specific points, the students have been moved out of the classroom and into a clinical setting where standardized patients represent the client in the case study. Providing this broader context for the psycho-social-economic dimensions of the health care delivery system has been well accepted by the students.

Despite the high student satisfaction with the course, only 1 percent of the total student population enrolls each semester. Why has enrollment not grown, despite student satisfaction? Why has there been limited interest by faculty in the various schools? Clearly, although interdisciplinary education remains the most significant aspect of being a model center (as we defined it), the concept had not become inculcated into the university culture as a widely shared value with corresponding institutional resources and support.

Clinical Case Competition

At the same time that the Core Curriculum Task Force was exploring the development of an interdisciplinary core curriculum, the UT-Houston president invited the institutional student governance organization to cosponsor an interdisciplinary Health Care Team Clinical Competition. The competition, initiated in 1993, is designed to enhance student knowledge about other health sciences disciplines and biomedical sciences and to promote an interdisciplinary approach to the delivery of health care.

The competition format makes it fun as well as educational. Three teams of students from all UT-Houston schools, and students from the University of Houston College of Pharmacy, Graduate School of Social Work, and, most recently, the Health Law Institute, are involved. They compete for awards of excellence before a live audience.

At an orientation meeting prior to the competition, the students are introduced to their teammates and presented with a hypothetical case prepared by a panel of faculty who also serve as judges. On the night of the competition, the students are given additional information about the case and asked to respond to several rounds of questions. A panel of faculty and other experts judge the quality of team responses. After the winning team is announced, the teams are asked to speak to the audience and with the other teams about their experiences as participants and the value of the competition.

Over the past six years, 238 students have volunteered to participate in the competition. Cases have ranged from patients with chronic illness to the health of a local community. By continually changing the focus of the case studies, different disciplines have led in the discourse during the team presentations each year.

Anecdotal comments from previous team members and faculty who examined the cases or asked questions have, for the most part, been extremely positive. Many team members have indicated they found the competition to be a valuable learning experience; several have returned to participate in following years. The faculty members, who themselves had to team up to develop cases, indicated that they have a better appreciation of the value of the team process and the expertise and knowledge contributed by other disciplines. A rewarding experience for all involved, the competition continues to be a visible and relatively simple means of introducing our students and faculty to an interdisciplinary approach.

REVISITING THE STRATEGIC IMPERATIVES

Since 1992, UT-Houston has accomplished a variety of program enhancements, reorganizations, downsizings, reallocations of funds, and creation of new programs consistent with our strategic directions. Over time, several of these goals have been fully achieved; one has been abandoned (the integration of basic sciences). The remaining original goals are well along their way to full accomplishment, and new strategic directions have been developed. But the goal to establish interdisciplinary education and activities as a comprehensive university attribute of the model health sciences university has not yet been fully realized.

In 1996, the university revisited the strategic imperatives set in 1992; during the intervening years, the university and schools had started implementing a variety of strategies to accomplish the strategic directions goals.

Because the "Frontiers" course was classroom based and did not at that time include a clinical component, leadership asked another team of faculty to look again at interdisciplinary training. This second task force reviewed existing models of interdisciplinary courses around the country and made recommendations to leadership on interdisciplinary training in the clinical setting.

According to their research, interdisciplinary training had been successful in a few settings, and the Task Force recommended that the university make an organizational commitment to developing such training. But although a small group of interdisciplinary partisans developed and continued to seek out support and venues for small pilot projects, there was no great impetus to move forward. Again, barriers including financing, optimal training sites, potential curriculum conflicts, and a number of other challenges stymied the effort.

WHY PERSIST?

Given the relative success of our interdisciplinary ventures, we grew somewhat complacent over time, satisfied that we could legitimately say that we had continuously pursued our strategic direction, offering students opportunities to learn with their colleagues. But the sense that we could do more persisted.

For many years, we have conducted what we call "strategic thinking sessions" each month during the academic year; they have been the primary means by which we refresh and extend our strategic thinking beyond conversations among administrators. Faculty, students, and other interested parties are specially invited to attend and provided with the topic and the sample questions to be discussed. The president hosts these sessions and is also a participant. The conversations are facilitated, but the primary intent is simply to talk about an issue—no particular outcome is sought. Typically, however, enthusiasm and support for a further exploration of the topic is generated. A number of task forces and other such groups have been stimulated by these discussions and gone on to make proposals for major institutional policy changes.

It appears that there has been a continuing motif in these discussions. In discussions of women's health, prime areas of research, the society and health initiatives, community outreach, spirituality, and other topics, the interdisciplinary theme recurs. We invariably conclude that approaching them from an interdisciplinary perspective will enhance such strategic endeavors. In other venues of discussion among faculty, students, and administration, interdisciplinary education continues to be depicted as a possible approach to any number of academic challenges: obtaining more clinical affiliates and preceptors; fostering more UT-Houston student interaction; and maximizing the allocation of dollars to enhancing technology around campus and beyond.

This theme and the development of a number of programs and activities demonstrating that students and faculty learn and teach effectively in an interdisciplinary environment bring us back time and again to the notion that interdisciplinary health professions education could well be a niche opportunity for this university. It could also provide a higher quality educational experience for our students.

Interdisciplinary achievements to date include the following:

- Establishment of an interdisciplinary Department of Health Informatics to develop and deliver graduate programs in health informatics. Students represent medicine, nursing, public health, dentistry, biomedical research, and allied health. The faculty also represents various health disciplines as well as expertise in informatics. Both master's and doctoral degrees will be offered.
- Establishment of a doctor of medicine/master of public health (MD/MPH) program as a joint effort between the Medical School and the School of Public Health.
- Establishment of a doctor of dental surgery/master of public health (DDS/MPH) dual degree and residency program.
- Enhancement of the master of science in nursing/master of public health (MSN/MPH) program as a joint degree; faculty from both schools collaborate in course delivery.
- Design and development of community-based, outreach efforts (Acres Homes Project and the Rusk Elementary Health Promotion Project) that involve faculty and students from all the health professions schools in service-learning activities.
- Extension of the UT-Houston Medicine/Public Health initiative in a number of projects relating to interdisciplinary and interprofessional teaching, research, and service. In particular, a group of students representing UT-Houston schools works each summer as an interdisciplinary team to conduct collaborative research and address curricular issues

related to the integration of public health concepts into the clinical disciplines.

Clearly the vision of "becoming the model health sciences university" has taken more shape and become more clearly defined in its strategic directions, but in terms of interdisciplinary education, more had to be done.

AN OPPORTUNITY TO LAUNCH
A FEASIBILITY STUDY

As an institution, UT-Houston is accredited by the Southern Association of Colleges and Schools (SACS). To retain full accreditation with SACS, we must, at ten-year intervals, demonstrate the excellence of our institution as compared to similar institutions. By assessing the academic and financial health of the university and demonstrating our institutional progress since the most recent institutional accreditation, we continue to be accredited. During each reaccreditation process, a year of institutional self-study is followed by the site visit of SACS representatives who review the institution and conduct the reaffirmation evaluation.

In the past at UT-Houston as well as at other institutions, the self-study effort has been focused on complying with each of the more than four hundred SACS evaluation criteria. This process has involved large numbers of faculty and administrators in a review of functional aspects of the organization aimed at assuring compliance. This type of self-study focuses primarily on the past. At its conclusion, the greatest benefit for the faculty, students, staff, and the institution is having confirmed the well-being of the institution.

When university leaders began planning the process of renewing accreditation, SACS extended to UT-Houston an opportunity to conduct an alternate self-study and use the self-study year as an alternative to the normal compliance-driven review of the organization. The alternate study had to be prospective, address a significant issue vital to the long-term well-being of the institution, serve a broad constituency within the institution, and involve and engage faculty in institutional improvement. Because we had made admirable inroads in the pursuit of interdisciplinary education but remained short of our goal, we concluded that a feasibility study of interdisciplinary education seemed a logical focus for the alternate study.

In view of the accomplishments noted above as well as a comprehensive environmental assessment in 1998, we saw this as an opportunity. Increasingly in a number of venues, our students and faculty declare a desire to learn and teach in a variety of health care delivery environments. The need to maintain an appropri-

144

ate patient base for training requires more and varied learning environments. Faculty work and students train now in organizations where many models of care depend on a team approach. UT-Houston faculty and academic leaders consistently underscore the potential we have to provide students with more and varied educational experiences; this potential is unmatched by comparable institutions. Within our own organization and with our close colleague institutions we have the capability to incorporate most of the members of the helping professions into an interdisciplinary experience. Could we actually take the needed steps to expose all students to the benefits inherent in interdisciplinary and interprofessional experiences?

Given this opportunity, UT-Houston is now conducting a feasibility study to determine the likelihood of implementing a required interdisciplinary learning experience for all students. This learning experience would incorporate both didactic content and practica; initial plans suggest a fall 2002 or 2003 start date.

It is important to emphasize that this study has emerged from an internally driven strategic intent. We are approaching the strategic intent as something the university must develop, support, and implement on its own if it is to be successful. Many health professions universities have developed a number of targeted, grant-funded interdisciplinary projects in the past; however, we did not see pursuing grant funding as a sound basis for launching such an extensive effort.

There is no foregone conclusion to this study. The university plans to use the process and outcomes of this study to make a policy decision about a proposed requirement for graduation. If the findings suggest that logistic, resource, organizational, and other challenges are so daunting as to preclude successful implementation, the institution will definitively close the issue and modify the strategic plan. If, on the other hand, the study's outcome suggests that interdisciplinary experiences are feasible given appropriate resources, policies, organizations, and technology, we will be able to redirect the energies and efforts expended by teams during this process toward the enhancement of existing academic programs. Or, we may decide that some subset of students, but not all students, will participate in formal interdisciplinary education.

Study Objectives

The expectations of the feasibility study are the following:
- To develop a firm institutional commitment to implement (or not to implement) a required interdisciplinary training experience for all UT-Houston students by the academic year 2003.
- To identify, address, and suggest approaches to challenges to implementation of interdisciplinary learning.

- To develop a plan for faculty development in skills/competencies required to teach in this milieu.
- To devise a model interdisciplinary curriculum.
- To conceive a financing plan for the model.

The Study Process

The Executive Team comprises the executive leadership of the university and the deans. Their role is to assure active and comprehensive support for the study from the faculty and staff in their schools; review the outcomes and recommendations of the study teams; deliberate the potential institutional policy change; determine whether or not to implement a required interdisciplinary learning experience; and, finally, to implement any associated changes of university policy, procedures, organizational configurations, and budgets.

The assistant vice president for planning, aided by the assistant vice president for academic affairs and their respective staff members, facilitates and coordinates the study as well as provides staff support to study teams. They schedule meetings, set agendas, and document proceedings; track and document team efforts and progress; use Web-based technology to support team activities; and produce all documents associated with the study.

Because the project focus is so wide ranging, the project is divided into a number of study teams. These teams address various aspects of the academic enterprise projected to experience the greatest impact from the findings. Teams have UT-Houston faculty, administrators, and students (when appropriate) representing the various health disciplines. Teams also include representatives from colleague institutions.

Organization of the Study

The study process aims to coordinate activities and share information continually and at appropriate times in each group's deliberations. Some teams have been scheduled to meet consistently over the academic year 1999, while others phase in and out of activity as appropriate. There are nine teams. Descriptions of their tasks follow.

1. Communication/marketing team—Identify, implement, and develop effective communication strategies to support the project and interdisciplinary processes at UT-Houston.

2. Content team—Propose an appropriate interdisciplinary curriculum model for possible implementation at UT-Houston.

3. Technology team—Develop a plan to facilitate and enhance the imple-

mentation of interdisciplinary experiences through the application of a variety of teaching, learning, and communications technologies.

4. Faculty team—Assess the impact of implementing a required interdisciplinary learning experience on faculty; propose organizational policy changes needed to overcome any barriers to faculty involvement; and describe faculty development programs needed to support implementation.

5. Student team—Assess the impact of implementing a required interdisciplinary learning experience on students and propose organizational policy changes needed to overcome any barriers.

6. Affiliates/training sites team—Propose a model of interdisciplinary education in clinical and/or community-based sites.

7. Organizational infrastructure team—Assess the resource requirements of the proposed model and propose alternative methods of financing the model.

8. Evaluation team—Design an evaluation plan for the model.

9. Synthesis team—Maintain consistent communication and information resources among all self-study groups; promote study coherence and consistency; and monitor and evaluate the project process.

The UT-Houston SACS Feasibility Study Web site (http://www.uth. tmc.edu/sacs/) includes every document, E-mail, chart, diagram, and other materials related to the project. Each team has its own Listserv application and E-mail archive so participants can engage each other on issues asynchronously and easily access any project communication.

As the project draws to a close and the teams each complete their charge, project managers and the synthesis team—as well as any others who want to participate—will synthesize and coalesce team outcomes into a final report to the Executive Committee. The decision-making process, based on the outcome of the study, was slated to start in September 1999.

In September 1998, we invited more than 150 faculty, students, and academic administrators from UT-Houston, along with a number of colleagues from the University of Houston, to participate in the study. One hundred forty-seven people accepted the invitation and approximately one hundred have remained consistently involved, with others participating as their teaching and clinical activities allow. This high degree of participation is fairly clear evidence of a willingness to address a topic of broad interest, even though there were and are skeptics about the value of interdisciplinary educational activities. It is also interesting to note that this university had never before brought together so many people from various schools and administrative units to work together on a project. As leaders and project managers, we anticipated a much higher degree of resistance or unwillingness to participate (primarily due to the intense demand for faculty time); we were astounded at not only the number of willing participants but also by their relative enthusiasm for the project.

We have devoted significant effort to communicating and clarifying the role of each team in the project as well as the roles of participants in those teams. The first major challenge for the facilitation team was to repeatedly, and in various ways, clarify and underscore that there was no predetermined intent to move forward with implementation of an interdisciplinary learning experience until the study was completed and the findings reviewed. The second challenge was to assure and reassure team members that they were not being asked to make decisions or recommendations as to the viability of new interdisciplinary courses.

A final challenge has been to sustain the perception that team members were not expected to become proselytizers or champions of interdisciplinary education. Not surprisingly, all three of these misperceptions continue to recur even in these late months of the project.

Definition of 'interdisciplinary education.' Much time in early team meetings was spent discussing both a common definition of interdisciplinary education and the assumptions upon which the work of the teams would be based. After reviewing the many varied definitions from the literature, the team agreed on the following working definition for the project.

> Interdisciplinary health professions education is a method of teaching and learning that integrates various disciplinary perspectives with curricular approaches that apply methodology and language to examine a central theme, issue, topic, or experience. More than a gathering of faculty or students from different health disciplines to learn and collaborate on a solution, it implies an interchange and blending of methods, information, knowledge, and ideas that result in a benefit to all participating disciplines by increasing their knowledge base and interpersonal skills for the good of the patient, the community, or the population.

Premise document. In an even more complicated process, teams reached consensus on operating assumptions, or a rationale, for this project. The procedure was complicated by the fact that many team members questioned the lack of documented evidence that interdisciplinary educational experiences produce positive, meaningful, and sustainable outcomes for students. Other team members felt that their own positive experiences as well as the anecdotal evidence of student satisfaction (and even enthusiasm) for these experiences was sufficient to provide a sound rationale for conducting the project.

Once we all agreed that we would continue to seek out evidence of positive

UT-Houston Rationale for Interdisciplinary Education

Interdisciplinary educational experiences during training can make UT-Houston students better practitioners in the evolving health care delivery environment and provide unique learning experiences that supplement their disciplinary education and training.

The commingling of students from various disciplines in shared learning environments pursuing shared learning objectives is a positive experience in and of itself and adds value to the educational experience at UT-Houston.

Faculty benefit from working with colleagues from other backgrounds in interdisciplinary pursuits, as well as with students of different backgrounds.

The evolving health care delivery environment and research environment require knowledge across the spectrum of health professions and biomedical research, skills in interpersonal communication and teamwork, and education and skills in discrete disciplines.

Knowledge of the expertise, competencies, and availability of other health and biomedical sciences pro-fessionals, as well as the ability to communicate effectively with those professionals, will benefit all UT-Houston students. If students learn early to work cooperatively with individuals with varying disciplinary perspectives, they are more likely to do so when they enter the health and biomedical sciences workforce.

With its array of disciplines and academic, research, and services programs, UT-Houston has a unique potential for developing and implementing interdisciplinary educational experiences.

Developing and implementing an interdisciplinary model for training health professionals will emphasize UT-Houston's unique qualities among academic health centers in this region.

Interdisciplinary approaches to many health care challenges, whether in clinical environments, community-based settings, or other venues, can result in improved health care as well as better integration of services to patients and populations, underscoring UT-Houston's goal of preparing highly qualified health care professionals for the State of Texas.

---

outcomes in the literature and continue to discuss these issues, the teams agreed on the following premises for the project. Since the time this document was accepted, there has been little or no revisiting of these issues.

Grappling with Content

The Content Team was charged with sketching a model of potential interdisciplinary activities for use by the other teams and subsequently refining and extending that model. This team was composed primarily of faculty who had served on curriculum committees in their schools. Unfortunately, this team was very slow to start, which hindered all the other teams. After two months, we galvanized this group by temporarily merging them with the Technology Team. Interestingly, even though the Technology Team is composed primarily of informatics enthusiasts and other "techies," they had many content ideas and were able to stimulate a move forward. At project midpoint, they had developed a draft model that they shared at our first retreat. The update of this model appears as table 1.

The Emerging Model

Table 1 began as a collaboration between the Content and Technology Teams, but all the other teams were invited to comment and suggest enhancement to the model. The curriculum is a trilevel experience best conceptualized as a spiral in which a student may move from a classroom experience, gaining foundation knowledge; to a simulation experience, using problem-based learning case studies; to a clinical application/practice experience requiring both technical and teamwork skills. It includes one required course and additional elective courses that will be integrated and articulated within the curriculum. Completion of credits in all three levels will merit a Certificate of Interdisciplinary Competence.

Embracing the Barriers

A phenomenon that we have come to call "embracing the barriers" has been a consistent factor in most team deliberations throughout the project. This concept is demonstrated as team members start integrating the notion of interdisciplinary education with the prospect of actually putting the model into effect. There has been no outright hostility toward the concept, nor has there been overt criticism or skepticism about its potential value. Rather, there is the nagging perception, based on team members' experiences in academe and at UT-Houston, that this notion—characterized as radical—will be stymied by the challenges or barriers that, over time, have affected most, if not all, innovations in health professions education. These include promotion, tenure, and other career development issues; compensation for teaching; reallocating resources from the status quo; curriculum committees; and so forth.

After hearing this litany of perceived barriers, the executive vice president for administration and finance at the university commented,

> I've been in higher education administration over twenty-five years and these are the same issues I've heard every time an innovation was discussed. We may never satisfactorily resolve these issues; the only thing we as a university community can do is acknowledge them, try to devise alternative ways to deal with them, and move forward!

After continuing over several months to deal with this phenomenon, pro-

Table 1
The UT-Houston Interdisciplinary Curriculum Model

	Level One **Acquisition of Foundation Knowledge and Tools**
Prototypical Experience	**Course** *required*
Title	**Foundations of Interdisciplinary Health Care Practice**
Purpose	To prepare students to practice from an interdisciplinary focus through development of team building, interpersonal communication, and conflict resolution skills necessary to function in a team environment; and through the acquisition, organization, and synthesis of information and decision making among a health care team to effectively address patient, family, and community health care issues.
Content	Health Concepts [roles, delivery systems, health and community, cultural aspects of health care, concepts of prevention and therapeutics, theory and practice of interdisciplinary care, etc.]; Team Organization Concepts [team function/roles, conflict resolution, etc.]; Information Gathering and Synthesis and Informatics [computer-assisted collaborative work and modalities used to support health care delivery at a distance].
Program Goals	Provide a broader understanding of health from a variety of perspectives. Identify current issues related to the effectiveness, efficiency, and equity of health care delivery; legal economic, social, and political dynamics in the health care delivery environment. Develop abilities to work productively and effectively in a team. Develop skills in accessing, synthesizing, and applying the health informational resources. Expose students to learning activities requiring an understanding of the diversity of human experience and its impact on their future roles as health care professionals.
Learning Experiences	Classroom instruction as well as such experiences as hospital rounds in teams, health fairs in community settings, team experiences, and group projects.
Evaluation Methods	*To be determined*
Optional Completion Credits	Students who can demonstrate that this course does not contribute to their career goals may choose electives in Levels 2 and 3.

Table 1 (continued)

Level Two
Development and Improvement of Skills Through Simulation

Prototypical Experience	**Problem-Based Case Studies** *elective*
Title	**Frontiers in Interdisciplinary Health Care**
Purpose	To demonstrate the interdisciplinary aspects of a number of major health problems and the potential for their optimal prevention and treatment through the combined competencies of graduates of each of the University of Texas-Houston Health Science Center Schools.
Content	Cases, typically based on actual cases, that feature a primary focus on a major health problem which is of concern to all health care disciplines; and have secondary foci involving issues relevant to the unique competencies of students and graduates of each school; and interdisciplinary issues such as prevention, ethics, nutrition, risk management, etc.
Program Goals	Provide opportunities to gain understanding/appreciation of roles and relationships among health professions.
	Provide shared/collaborative learning experiences to develop abilities to work productively and effectively among a group of professionals.
	Develop skills in accessing, synthesizing, and applying the vast array of health informational resources.
	Establish a common basis of problem-solving experience through working through a case.
	Provide opportunities to demonstrate effective teamwork behaviors.
Learning Experiences	PBL (problem-based learning) cases initially developed as a live group, and later as a "virtual group," i.e., meetings take place in a computer network environment that provides for shared data, synchronous meetings/discussion, and asynchronous discussion.
Evaluation Methods	*To be determined*
Optional Completion Credits	Students may choose to enroll in other interdisciplinary courses as an alternative.

Table 1 (continued)

Level Three
Application Through Service Teams

Prototypical Experience	Rotations or practica; collaborative projects *elective*
Title	**The Practice of Interdisciplinary Health Care in a Health Care and/or Community Setting**
Purpose	To provide practice in interdisciplinary health care teams.
Content	Projects generated from a variety of "real-life" settings such as community health centers, special needs clinics, health departments, school-based clinics, mobile health care units, etc., where students and faculty work collaboratively on health issues from a population perspective as they affect an individual, a family or group, a community, or particular population.
Program Goals	Provide opportunities to apply understanding/appreciation of roles and relationships among teams of health professionals.
	Provide shared/collaborative learning experiences to develop abilities to work productively and effectively among a group of professionals and with members of the community.
	Establish a common basis of experience through working with individuals, families, and groups in community settings geared toward a greater understanding of the diversity of human experience and the impact on their future roles as health care professionals.
Learning Experiences	Interdisciplinary student/faculty teams follow and interact with an individual, family, group, community, and so forth for a specified length of time and collaboratively define and pursue a project of mutual benefit to the students and their collaborators. Teamwork will be supported by a computer network and software environment to enable collaborative work.
Evaluation Methods	*To be determined*
Optional Completion Credits	Students may choose to work as a group, sponsored by a faculty member, that represents interdisciplinary, collaborative work in other than clinical settings [e.g., research].

ject facilitators coalesced all the perceived barriers from each team and documented possible alternatives. This document has been widely discussed and shaped over
several months. Table 2 reflects the current status of that effort.

The Retreat

Midway through the feasibility study in January 1999, we held a retreat at a local
conference center for all project team members. We invited DeWitt C. Baldwin,
Jr., MD, scholar-in-residence and senior associate at the Institute for Ethics of the
American Medical Association, as our keynote speaker. For most of his distin-
guished career, Dr. Baldwin has been involved in interdisciplinary health professions education and written extensively on the topic. We disseminated one of his
articles (Baldwin 1996) to every team member before the retreat. We planned the
agenda so that Dr. Baldwin would begin the session with his remarks about the
concept and the status of interdisciplinary education from his perspective.
Subsequently, each team presented an overview of its progress.

Dr. Baldwin offered his comments on all these reports at the end and facilitated an open question-and-answer session. Notes and exhibits from the retreat
were posted on the Web site. Ninety-three team members participated, as well as
five of the six deans of UT-Houston schools. An E-mail survey of all participants
reflected an extremely high degree of satisfaction with the retreat. We plan a similar retreat as the project draws to a close.

Focus Groups

Several teams, but particularly the Student Team, felt strongly that they needed
more participation of students in their deliberations. Student participation on the
teams is affected by their class schedules, and the students who are participating
in the project are already known to be proponents of interdisciplinary education.
Since roughly 350 current students have participated in either the Health Care
Team Competition or the Frontiers course, the team initially conducted focus
groups with those students. These focus groups drew approximately thirty participants; this is a small number of participants given the size of the cohort, but the
team felt that it was sufficient for meaningful input.

The conversations stimulated by these questions were transcribed, shared,
and analyzed by the team members. Representative comments of this group of
admittedly self-selected interdisciplinary students were positive toward developing
a greater institutional emphasis on interdisciplinary experiences.

These comments bolstered the Student Team's search for providing the
benefit of interdisciplinary experiences in other ways. In particular, the barriers to
student participation in interdisciplinary activities have been better clarified for

Table 2

Challenges to Interdisciplinary Education and the Alternatives

Challenges	Alternatives
Academic calendars	• Integrate UT-Houston calendars (and catalogs) into one calendar (or, at most two: academic and professional). • Schedule interdisciplinary courses and activities in the core months of a semester.
Academic requirements	• Develop a distinct grading system that would allow any school to use a conversion protocol to translate interdisciplinary grades into the grading system of that school. • Faculty develop a consistent grading system across campus for all schools.
Academic reward structure	• Recruit faculty to interdisciplinary activities whose primary activities are not directed toward promotion/tenure. • Particularly with junior faculty who would like to teach in this environment, assure that interdisciplinary work is linked to his/her faculty development plan in his/her primary department. • Create separate merit pool related to interdisciplinary activities. • Continue to promote efforts for Appointment/Promotion/Tenure Committees to recognize the expanded view of scholarship particularly as it is demonstrated in interdisciplinary activities.
Clinical/practica sites where interdisciplinary teams practice	• This is a significant challenge; current plans would make these types of opportunities elective only. • Forge alliances with external organizations that employ interdisciplinary approval.
Communication issues; advertising/marketing the courses	• Coordinate program communications among the schools through the interdisciplinary organizational unit. • Coordinate program marketing (catalogs, orientation, etc.) among the schools through the interdisciplinary organizational unit.
Cost issues for students, e.g., tuition for additional course	• Add a required interdisciplinary course at the expense of one elective course. Total credit hours needed to graduate would remain the same. • Devise a means of providing the course at no cost to the student.
Disciplinary/departmental organization and structure. (The accepted premise is that interdisciplinary work cannot be dependent on volunteer faculty.)	• Create a separate organizational entity for interdisciplinary activities; allocate faculty FTEs to that organization. • Reimburse school/departments for faculty FTEs allocated to interdisciplinary unit. • Devote significant implementation planning to faculty communication and development.
Disciplinary and professional traditions and cultures	• Reinforce the fact that a major goal of interdisciplinary activities is to mediate differences.

Table 2 (continued)

Challenges	Alternatives
Evaluation	• Design a rigorous, programmatic evaluation plan for any interdisciplinary courses.
Faculty development	• Ensure that the interdisciplinary organizational unit collaborates with each school's faculty development efforts. • Develop courses specifically related to interdisciplinary teaching and evaluation. • Provide consultation to department heads regarding faculty development plans involving interdisciplinary work.
Fiscal and faculty resources	• Fiscal wherewithal probably lies within current operating budgets; thus funds could be reallocated. • Assign interdisciplinary curriculum highest priority for state funds request in 2001. • Redeploy faculty from current teaching assignments.
Geographical separation (10 academic buildings within the Texas Medical Center)	• Provide universal parking privileges for interdisciplinary faculty. • Assure that faculty time agreement includes not only accommodation for teaching time but also class preparation and travel time.
Insufficient interdisciplinary curriculum offerings	• With full implementation of the curricula plan (Levels 1-3), there will be many and varied opportunities. • Publicize current interdisciplinary curriculum offerings. (During this project we have realized there are already many opportunities for this approach to content. Faculty and students are not aware of them.)
Insufficient interdisciplinary faculty	• Define competencies desired in interdisciplinary faculty and develop/offer training in those skills. • Recruit initially from PBL-trained faculty. • Seek preceptors from the practice community to assist in interdisciplinary teaching. • Use fourth-year medical students, PhD, and DSN students as facilitators.
Interdisciplinary role models	• This is a significant challenge; underscores the need to further investigate development of a model interdisciplinary clinical practice.
Leadership and administrative support	• If UT-Houston leadership goes forward with planning for implementation of interdisciplinary activities, there will be support at the university and school administration levels. • The deans will work with department heads to assure support at that level.
Levels of student preparation and maturity	• Categorize whatever courses, rotations, practica, etc., are developed and implemented in terms of appropriate student readiness for that material.

Table 2 (continued)

Challenges	Alternatives
	• Establish pre/post assessments and relate to student performance in year one and modify prerequisites if needed. • Monitor, during registration, class mix in terms of student preparation and maturity in terms of students' own advisers. • Establish all interdisciplinary courses as competency based.
Licensing and accrediting bodies and requirements	• Review accreditation requirements and document potential problem areas, if any. (Completed) • Include interdisciplinary courses in school accreditation processes as appropriate.
Legal and legislative definitions (e.g., scope of practice)	• Seek affiliation with health care delivery systems/sites where covered lives are capitated or represent a defined population (on the assumption that these issues have been resolved). • Defer any significant analysis of this issue until implementation planning begins if the project goes forward.
Logistics	• Hold the interdisciplinary organizational unit responsible for all the logistical elements. • Hold classes at every academic building on campus. • Offer flexible schedules including a variety of options, e.g., monthly, weekly, early mornings, evenings, weekends. • Establish a faculty advisory board for the interdisciplinary organizational unit. • Charge the interdisciplinary faculty with leadership of faculty recruitment efforts.
Power dispositions and territorial imperatives	• This will change only as interdisciplinary activity becomes more commonplace.
Priorities—both institutional and those of the schools	• If this project proceeds toward implementation, the institution must declare it one of its highest priorities for the 2002–2003 biennium.
Promotion and tenure considerations	• Create an interdisciplinary career path and recruit junior faculty after initial implementation of the Level 1 course. • Continue to promote efforts for Appointment, Promotion, and Tenure Committees to recognize the scholarship of teaching as it is demonstrated in interdisciplinary activities.
Recognition/reward	• Develop a means of recognizing the contributions of the faculty who participate in interdisciplinary teaching including both tangible and intangible rewards.

Table 2 (continued)

Challenges	Alternatives
Recruitment	• Create a separate organizational entity for interdisciplinary activities; allocate faculty FTEs to that organization. • Reimburse school/departments for faculty FTEs allocated to interdisciplinary unit.
Resistance to change	• An intrinsic part of the change process—accept it and continue to move forward. • Create seed grants to faculty for the development of courses. • Continue leadership efforts to stimulate interest in teaching, including faculty development plans.
Reimbursement mechanisms and schedules for clinical professions	• Include on-site interdisciplinary training activities as part of negotiation and renegotiation of affiliation and other such agreements. • Focus majority of interdisciplinary clinical rotations in clinical sites where UT-Houston controls clinic management. • Create an interdisciplinary clinic run by UT-Houston. • Seek affiliation with health care delivery systems/sites where covered lives are capitated or represent a defined population. • Influence state legislation regarding reimbursements of interdisciplinary teams for care.
Scholarship	• Continue to promote efforts for Appointment, Promotion, and Tenure Committees to recognize the scholarship of teaching as it is demonstrated in interdisciplinary activities. • ID organizational unit should be initially responsible for assisting faculty with grant opportunities and publishing associated with interdisciplinary activities.
Time commitment	• Create a separate organizational entity for interdisciplinary activities; allocate faculty FTEs to that organization. • Reimburse school/departments for faculty FTEs allocated to interdisciplinary unit.

Note: FTE=full-time equivalent; PBL=problem-based learning.

members of this team, many of whom are academic administrators.

In the second phase of the student focus group effort, we have conducted similar focus groups with students who have not participated in interdisciplinary activities. Working with the student affairs offices in each school, we randomly selected approximately three hundred students as a cohort and invited them in writing, E-mails, phone calls, and so forth to attend. These focus groups are in progress now.

The Clinical Affiliates and Training Sites Team determined early in the process that rather than conduct surveys, they would seek information from Houston-area health care providers, primarily those in integrated health care delivery systems. This approach was designed to help the team analyze where we might try to create interdisciplinary clinical experiences. Plans were also developed to host several such focus groups consisting of executives of the major health care systems, clinic administrators, and various groups of patients. The team was careful to select and recruit the appropriate people for each group. These sessions were conducted throughout May 1999.

The Clinical Affiliates and Training Sites Team is also designing an optimal interdisciplinary training site. Members hope to find a local partner who might sponsor a pilot project for an interdisciplinary team of faculty and students in a local clinical site.

Other teams not mentioned here—e.g., Communication, Organizational Infrastructure, Evaluation, and Synthesis—have been making expected progress and will produce their deliverables in the final phases of the project.

LESSONS FOR LEADERS

It is difficult to draw conclusions about which of our strategies have succeeded beyond our expectations and which we would redesign. However, several aspects of this project are readily apparent even as we continue to pursue our project goals.

Focus on Group Process

As we have worked with teams, we have repeatedly been reassured that our initial project design and intent has promoted success. Our decision to drive the project from our mission and our strategic advantage was sound. If we had approached our effort as a project to attract funding to the university or for some other more restrictive reason, we might not have been able to maintain interest or sustain activity. We may also have been forced to adapt our primary focus to that of any potential funding agency.

It is also clear that the leaders can never sufficiently reinforce the purpose, goals, and expected outcomes of such an effort. We thought we were doing this adequately as the project began; we learned over time that we must keep task-oriented groups focused upon the big picture.

The comprehensive involvement of faculty, students, administrators, and stakeholders has served us well. It is clear that our project's success so far stems primarily from the way it has brought individuals from all aspects of our university together, focusing on a common topic of interest and purpose. The inclusion of skeptics along with adherents has added to the rigor of the process and seems to have promoted a more open-minded reception from those not involved in the project.

One important approach to forming teams is avoiding the danger of including too many like-minded people or people with common backgrounds on any one team. In several instances, particularly those related to evaluation and content, the predominance of similar perspectives may have hampered exploration of possible options.

Project management and the devotion of considerable time and effort from senior university administrators and their support staffs has done much to sustain progress over time and to keep the process moving forward. Most important perhaps, has been their ability to synthesize and coordinate the efforts of one team with others. At the retreat, Dr. Baldwin noted that he had never before seen such commitment from a university administration to provide leadership and support in such an effort.

We heard early from students who have pursued interdisciplinary activities that one must attend to group processes as a first step among student groups. We have also found that we cannot assume that faculty and administrators have already mastered working in a group as a team. If we were to begin again, we would spend much more time in the early meetings working on precepts for interaction within and among groups. Group efficiency has, over time, worked itself out, but we would have saved time and communication breakdowns had we dealt with this early in the study process.

It is also important to explore the semantics of a particular discussion from various disciplinary perspectives. Exploring such terms as health, disease, evidence-based, interprofessional, and multiprofessional from the various clinical perspectives might have facilitated easier communication early in the project. We had assumed that the faculty interpreted such terms much more similarly than they actually did. (These semantics discussions are invariably lively and stimulating in and of themselves.)

Also critical is devoting time to establishing a common ground as a rationale for proceeding with this effort, particularly where there is little research-based evidence to support benefits of interdisciplinary experiences for students. Had we not spent much time and work in this aspect of project development, we might not have been able to proceed at all.

Commit to the Process

The visible commitment of the president and other executive leaders, particularly the deans, is critical to the success of such an endeavor. We have been openly advocating interdisciplinary activities for students through our tenure, and feel that willingness to step forward as leaders of the study has promoted what seems to be a successful project. Implicit in this willingness is a commitment to letting the process unfold while, at the same time, withholding preliminary judgment. On the other hand, we have made it clear that this is a feasibility study; this is not an implementation-planning project. We need and want the involvement of even more faculty in the process once we start deliberating whether or not to go forward.

Undeniably, part of the willingness of faculty to participate is attributable to the fact that a feasibility study is a much more stimulating experience than a compliance review. But, we feel confident that so many faculty committed to this project because they know it is supported from the top of the organization, and they are pleased to devote university-citizenship time to a project of this nature.

Clarify and Reinforce Purpose

Although the following may seem patently obvious, the devotion of time early in the process to clarify exactly what the expectations of leadership and other constituents are is time well spent. In our case, we continually discussed and explored why this project was intended to conduct a feasibility study—not to plan implementation.

It is also critical that a project like this be driven by solid, mission-based intentions rather than in response to an external driver. The many compelling and often competing priorities within our university meant that to approach implementation of interdisciplinary experiences as yet another new program might have quashed the initiative before it could ever get to the forefront of university discourse. By seizing an opportunity where we have been forced to devote significant amounts of faculty and administrative time to a reflective process and grounding the stimulus for the project in our mission, we have a greater potential for project acceptance.

In planning the project, we considered process goals as well as programmatic goals and viewed them as equally important. No matter what the outcome, the project has become one more way to bring this university together in a common cause. We spent a great deal of time talking with the university leaders about what we hoped the process will generate in terms of collegiality, collaboration, and joint commitment to university goals.

Support the Process

As the project was designed, we felt that it was imperative to earmark funds for support of the process; we allocated both funds for project facilitation as well as staff to support the project. The project infrastructure enables participants to devote their time to interactions with each other on an intellectual level rather than on more mundane tasks.

In projects such as ours, as many varied perspectives as feasible fuel discourse. We have included a variety of faculty: clinicians, basic science teachers and researchers, clinical researchers, et cetera. We have also included faculty from our partner institutions. Students from all our schools serve on teams. Academic administrators participate on teams as do administrators from such areas as development, administrative computing, student services, budget, educational outreach, community outreach, and governmental relations. We have also sought perspectives from alumni, members of our development board, and other UT System institutions. Managing all this input remains a challenge, but widespread participation has been a first-order project goal in and of itself.

Seek Partnerships

Although we have within our own university representation of the primary health disciplines, we do not have them all. We, therefore, sought out potential participants from pharmacy, optometry, allied health professions, and health care administration. We also sought out representatives of social work, education, and chaplaincy. Most of these programs reside at the University of Houston, which describes itself as Texas's premier metropolitan research and teaching institution. With over 33,000 students, this university offers a full range of undergraduate, graduate, and professional degrees (with the exception of most health-related professions). The University of Houston is a strategic partner in the city and region. Any project relating to interdisciplinary health professions education should include participants from complementary disciplines.

Similarly, with more than two hundred clinical affiliates, we felt strongly that we should include representatives of our primary or targeted affiliates; thus, the city and county health departments as well as other health care providers are also represented on the project.

On the other hand, we continue to reinforce that this is a UT-Houston effort and is linked to our strategic development. Attempting to include every potential stakeholder as a partner at this time would drain project resources and distract from our mission focus. We maintain a delicate balance between seeking participation and input to our process while maintaining focus.

Although we are already impressed by the effort of our faculty and staff to think creatively and innovatively about our potential as an academic health center with an interdisciplinary perspective, we are eager to see the tangible outcomes of this project. Whether or not we will proceed to launch a university-wide interdisciplinary curriculum remains to be seen. Based upon this project to date, however, we can say that both current and future initiatives aimed at enhancing the education of our students through interdisciplinary means will be received with much greater enthusiasm and more consideration than was possible before.

By summer in the year 2000, the University of Texas-Houston Health Science Center will have thoroughly explored innovative and intriguing models of interdisciplinary health professions education. We will also have had lively discussions about whether or not to go forward with this model and look forward to sharing more about our project in the future with our colleagues in academic health centers across North America.

REFERENCES

Abernathy, D.J. 1999. Leading edge learning: Two views. *Training & Development* March:40–42.

Alexander, G.C., B. Fera, and R. Ellis. 1996. From the students: Learning continuous improvement by doing it. *Joint Commission Journal on Quality Improvement* (22)3:198–205.

Arcangelo, V., M. Fitzgerald, D. Carroll, and J.D. Plum. 1996. Collaborative care between nurse practitioners and primary care physicians. *Primary Care* (23)1:103–13.

Baggs, J.G., S.A. Ryan, C. E. Phelps, J.F. Richeson, and J.E. Johnson. 1992. The association between interdisciplinary collaboration and patient outcomes in a medical intensive care unit. *Heart & Lung* (21)1:18–24.

Baggs, J.G., and M.H. Schmitt. 1988. Collaboration between nurses and physicians. *IMAGE: Journal of Nursing Scholarship* (20)3:145–49.

Baldwin, Jr., D.C. 1996. Some historical notes on interdisciplinary and interprofessional education and practice in health care in the USA. *Journal of Interprofessional Care* (10)2:173–87.

———. 1998. The case for interdisciplinary education. *In Mission Management: A New Synthesis,* Vol. 2. E.R. Rubin, ed. Washington: Association of Academic Health Centers, pp. 151–64.

Baldwin, Jr., D.C., and M.A. Baldwin. 1979. Interdisciplinary education and health team training: A model for learning and service. In *Medical Education Since 1960: Marching to a Different Drummer,* A.D. Hunt and L.E. Weeks. East Lansing: Michigan State Foundation, pp. 190-221.

——— 1981. Education for teamwork in primary health care. In *Approaches to Teaching Primary Health Care,* H.J. Knopke, and N.L. Diekelmann. St. Louis: Mosby, pp. 176-95.

Baldwin Jr., D.C., and R.A.W. Tsukuda. 1984. Interdisciplinary teams. In *Geriatric Medicine*, Vol. 2 *(Fundamentals of Geriatric Care)*, C.W. Cassel, and J.R. Walsh. New York: Springer-Verlag, pp. 421-35.

Balestreire, J. 1996. The Pennsylvania Local Interdisciplinary Team Journal into Collaborative Learning and Community Health Improvement. *The Joint Commission Journal on Quality Improvement* (22)3:171–77.

Batalden, P.B. 1996. Stakeholders and reflections on improving health professions education: What's next. *The Joint Commission Journal on Quality Improvement* (22)3:229-36.

Blumenthal, D., E.G. Campbell, and J. Weissman. 1997. The social missions of academic health centers. *New England Journal of Medicine* (337)21:1550–53.

Bolton, L.B., C.A. Georges, V. Hunter, V. Long, and R. Wray. 1998. Community health collaboration models for the 21st century. *Nursing Administration Quarterly* (22)3:6–17.

Boyer, M.H. 1997. A decade's experience at Tufts with a four-year combined curriculum in medicine and public health. *Academic Medicine* (72)4:269–75.

Donaldson, S.K. 1998. The growth of collaborative and interdisciplinary research. In *Creating Nursing's Future: Issues, Opportunities, and Challenges*, E.J. Sullivan. St. Louis: Mosby, pp. 271–78.

Evans, J.R. 1992. The "health of the public" approach to medical education. *Academic Medicine* 67:719–23.

Finocchio, L.J., J.M. Coffman, C.M. Dower, and E.H. O'Neil. 1996. Physicians and nurse practitioners—old conflicts and new opportunities. *Western Journal of Medicine* (165)4:246–48.

Gelmon, S.B. 1996. Can educational accreditation drive interdisciplinary learning in the health professions? *The Joint Commission Journal on Quality Improvement* (22)3:213–22.

Gordon, P.R., L. Carlson, A. Chessman, M.L. Kundrat, P.S. Moran, and L.A. Headrick. 1996. A multisite collaborative for the development of interdisciplinary education in continuous improvement for health professions students. *Academic Medicine* (71)9:973–78.

Hammick, M. 1998. Interprofessional education: Concept, theory, and application. *Journal of Interprofessional Care* (12)3:323–32.

Harris, D.L., S.M. Starnaman, R.C. Henry, and J.C. Bland. 1998. Alternative approaches to program evaluation. *Academic Medicine* (73)10:S13–15.

Headrick, L.A., M. Knapp, D. Neuhamsed, S. Gelman, L. Newman, D. Quinn, and A. Baker. 1996. Working from upstream to improve health care: The IHI Interdisciplinary Professional Education Collaborative. *The Joint Commission Journal on Quality Improvement* (22)3:149–64.

Hewison, A., and J. Sim. 1998. Managing interprofessional working: using codes of ethics as a foundation. *Journal of Interprofessional Care* 12(3):309–21.

Holmes, D.E., ed. 1997. *Interdisciplinary Education as a Prelude to Interdisciplinary Practice (or Vice Versa)*. Washington: Association of Academic Health Centers.

Hughes, L., and J. Lucas. 1997. An evaluation of problem-based learning in the multiprofessional education curriculum for the health professions. *Journal of Interprofessional Care* (11)1:77–88.

Ivey, S.L., K.S. Brown, Y. Teske, and D. Silverman. 1988. A model for teaching about interdisciplinary practice in health care settings. *Journal of Allied Health* (17)3:189–5.

Kahn, R. J., and D. J. Prager. 1994. Interdisciplinary collaborations are a scientific and social imperative. *The Scientist* July 11:12.

Kelly, K.C., D.G. Huber, A. Johnson, J. C. McCloskey, and M. Maas. 1994. The medical outcomes study: a nursing perspective. *Journal of Professional Nursing* (10)4:209–16.

Kovacich, J. 1996. Interdisciplinary team training on the information superhighway. *Journal of Interprofessional Care* (10)2:111–19.

Langley, A.E., C.A. Maurana, G.L. LeRoy, S.M. Ahmed, and C.M. Harmon. 1998. Developing a community-academic health center: Strategies and lessons learned. *Journal of Interprofessional Care* (12)3:273–77.

Larson, E.L. 1995. New rules for the game: Interdisciplinary education for health professionals. *Nursing Outlook* (43)4:180-85.

Lindeke, L.L., and D.E. Block. 1998. Maintaining professional integrity in the midst of interdisciplinary collaboration. *Nursing Outlook* September/October:213–17.

Lurie, N. 1996. Preparing physicians for practice in managed care environments. *Academic Medicine* (71)10:1044–49.

Maurana, C., K. Goldberg, J.C. Swart, K.D. Glass, G. Goldman, and A.E. Langley. 1997. How a community-academic partnership serves as a force for change in health care and health professions education. *Journal of Health Care for the Poor and Underserved* (8)1:5–17.

Mellor, M.J., K.D. Davis, and C.F. Capello. 1997. Stages of development in the life of an academic interdisciplinary team in geriatrics. *Gerontology & Geriatrics Education* (18)2:3–36.

Moore, S.M., F. Alemi, L.A. Headrick, F. Hekelman, D. Neuhauser, J. Novotny, and A.D. Flowers. 1996. Interdisciplinary learning in the continuous improvement of health care: four perspectives. *The Joint Commission Journal on Quality Improvement* (22)3:165–87.

Neuhauser, D., and L. Norman. 1996. Accepting the Galvin challenge: Increasing efficiency and productivity in health professions education. *The Joint Commission Journal on Quality Improvement* (22)3:223–27.

O'Toole, M.T. 1992. The interdisciplinary team: Research and education. *Holistic Nursing Practice* (6)2:76–83.

Parsell, G., and J. Bligh. 1999. The development of a questionnaire to assess the readiness of health care students for interprofessional learning (RIPLS). *Medical Education* 33: 95–100.

Roemer, M. 1999. Genuine professional doctor of public health the world needs. *Image: Journal of Nursing Scholarship* (11)1:43–44.

Satin, D.G. 1994. A conceptual framework for working relationships among disciplines and the place of interdisciplinary education and practice: Clarifying muddy waters. *Gerontology & Geriatrics Education* (14)3:3-24.

Smith, M., J. Barton, and J. Baxter. 1996. An innovative, interdisciplinary educational experience in field research. *Nurse Educator* (21)2:27–30.

Spitzer, W.O. 1975. Issues for team delivery and interdisciplinary education: A Canadian perspective. *Journal of Medical Education* (50)12, part 2:117-21.

Swanson, E.A.A., C.M. Taylor, A.M. Valentine, and A.M. McCart. 1998. The integrated health professions education program seminar. *Nurse Educator* (23)2:18–20.

Taylor-Seehafer, M. 1998. Point view: Nurse-physician collaboration. *Journal of American Academy of Nurse Practitioners* (10)9:387–91.

Tresolini, C.P., D.A. Shugars, and L.S. Lee. 1995. Teaching an integrated approach to health care: Lessons from five schools. *Academic Medicine* (70)8:665–70.

Wahlstrom, O., I. Sanden, and M. Hammer. 1997. Multiprofessional education in the medical curriculum. *Medical Education* 31: 425–29.

Waite, M.S., J.O. Harker, and L. I. Misserman. 1994. Interdisciplinary team training and diversity: Problems, concepts, and strategies. *Gerontology & Geriatrics Education* (15)1:65–82.

Walker, P.H., J. Baldwin, D.C. Baldwin, Jr., J.J. Fitzpatrick, S. Ryan, R. Bulger, H. DeBasio, C. Hanson, R. Harran, J. Johnson-Paulson, M. Kelley, B. Lacey, M.J. Ladden, C. Mclaughlin, L. Selker, D. Sluyter, and N. Vanselow. 1998. Building community: Developing skills for interprofessional health. *Nursing Outlook* (46)2:88–9.

Weiss, S.J., and H.P. Davis. 1985. Validity and reliability of the collaborative practice scales. *Nursing Research* 34:299–305.

Wieczorek, R.R., E.A. Pennington, and S.K. Fields. 1976. Interdisciplinary education: A model for the resocialization of faculty. *Nursing Forum* (15)3:224–37.

Wilkes, M.S., R. Usatine, S. Slavin, and J.R. Hoffman. 1998. Doctoring: University of California, Los Angeles. *Academic Medicine* (73)1:32–40.

Zungolo, E. 1994. Interdisciplinary education in primary care: The challenge. *Nursing & Health Care* (15)6:288–92.

———1998. Interdisciplinary Practice and Education. In *Creating Nursing's Future: Issues, Opportunities, and Challenges*, J. Sullivan. St. Louis: Mosby, pp. 306–16.